The
BIRDWATCHER'S
NOTEBOOK

The
BIRDWATCHER'S
NOTEBOOK

Peter Slater

WELDON
PUBLISHING

Sydney • Hong Kong • Chicago • London

Distributed by Gary Allen Pty Ltd
9 Cooper Street, Smithfield, NSW 2164

A Kevin Weldon Production
Published by Weldon Publishing
a division of Kevin Weldon & Associates Pty Limited
372 Eastern Valley Way, Willoughby, NSW 2068,
Australia

First published 1988

Typeset in Australia by Savage Type Pty Ltd, Brisbane
Printed in Singapore by Kyodo-Shing Loong Printing
Pte Ltd

National Library of Australia Cataloguing-in-
Publication Data

Slater, Peter, 1932– .
The birdwatcher's notebook.

Includes index.
ISBN 0 947116 61 3.

1. Birds — Australia — Identification.
I. Title.

598.2994

Editor: Lesley Dow
Designer: Warren Penney

Front cover (from left to right, top to bottom): King Parrot, Blue-faced Honeyeater, Common Myna, Mistletoebird, Eclectus Parrot — male (green) and female, Wompoo Fruit-Dove, Yellow-bellied Sunbird, Common Starling.

CONTENTS

INTRODUCTION

There are some among us who are born with a passion for birds and who spend their time — much of which should be employed more gainfully — watching birds. Nobody has satisfactorily explained the origin of this ornithophilia — various theories suggest that it could be either subliminal hunting or an overdeveloped aesthetic sense or an Icarus syndrome, a desire to fly. Whatever its cause, there appears to be a 'bird-appreciation gene' somewhere among our chromosomes. It often skips generations, but lies latent in many of us until triggered by some fortunate juxtaposition of circumstances. Those who take up birdwatching in maturity are at some disadvantage compared to those who, growing up with birds, learn the tricks of observation very early in childhood when eyes are sharpest. But the seemingly miraculous ability to see birds everywhere can be learned even late in life.

It has been speculated that birds may have evolved from a group of small, hollow-boned dinosaurs known as coelurosaurs. Coelurosaurs were probably warm blooded and there is a likelihood that some species developed a down-like covering to help regulate body temperature. Through the

Fig. 1
Speculative reconstruction of a coelurosaur — Coelurus.

Fig. 2
Archaeopteryx, one of the feathered coelurosaurs.

course of evolution, the down probably developed further into feathers, which were more efficient for temperature regulation and, almost incidentally, made flight possible. It is feasible that feathers were also responsible for keeping eggs warm during the period of the Earth's temperature instability that resulted in the extinction of those dinosaurs that laid unprotected eggs. Certainly, modern birds still retain much in common anatomically with coelurosaurs and as John McLoughlin writes, 'We are forced to the conclusion that birds are no more nor less than dinosaurs, and that their classification outside [the dinosaurs] makes no more sense than would classifying bats outside [the mammals] because they can fly! . . . This point of view, of course, adds considerably to the enchantment of ornithology; . . . it shows that the loveliness of bird life is an echo of an even greater beauty, that of the whole of dinosaur biology of which birds are the only surviving expressions.' — John C. McLoughlin, *Archosauria* (Viking Press, 1977).

The feature that makes birds unique is the possession of feathers. They generally cover the body in tracts and may number as many as 25 000 in swans to less than 1000 in hummingbirds, providing insulation and making flight possible.

There are four kinds of feathers:

Contour feathers These cover the body and form the shape of the bird. They include the flight feathers, tail feathers and body feathers. Names given to different tracts of feathers are shown in Figures 3 and 4. Many birds have modified contour feathers; some examples are plumes used in display, for example, egrets; reduced and stiffened primaries that produce a whistling sound in flight, for example, Crested Pigeon; hair-like bristles around the eyes or about the gape, for example, harriers and flycatchers; stiffened tail feathers used either as

Fig. 3

Feather tracts (Richard's Pipit): 1 crown, 2 forehead (front), 3 bill, 4 chin, 5 lore, 6 throat, 7 chest, 8 breast, 9 lesser wing coverts, 10 median wing coverts, 11 greater wing coverts, 12 primary coverts, 13 belly, 14 thigh, 15 tarsus, 16 tail (retrices), 17 primaries, 18 secondaries, 19 scapulars, 20 mantle, 21 nape, 22 ear coverts.

support or in display, for example, Musk Duck, swifts and log-runners; compact net-like feathers over the earholes to enhance hearing ability, for example, barn owls.

Down feathers These underlie the contour feathers and are soft and filamentous. They are particularly abundant on waterbirds such as grebes, petrels, pelicans and ducks but are absent on emus, cassowaries and adult Painted Snipe. Many ducks pluck down from their bodies to line their nests. Down is also found on many fledgling birds; each down feather is pushed out by a developing contour feather. In young birds of prey, a second coat of down grows — about two weeks before the contour feathers appear.

Filoplumes These are hair-like feathers usually covered by the contour feathers, but visible in breeding cormorants, particularly on the head and thighs.

Powder-down feathers These are continuously growing down feathers whose tips break off as a fine powder. They are found in only a few groups of birds, for example, egrets, herons, bitterns and woodswallows.

Feathers occur in an incredible variety of colours. Two sorts of coloration occur in birds — chemical and structural. Chemical coloration is caused by pigments, which absorb part of the spectrum and reflect the remainder as the colours we see. Red, orange and yellow colours are mainly produced by carotenoids, occurring in bare skin as well as in feathers. These pigments are fat-soluble and are extracted from food. Flamingoes, for example, lose their pink coloration if deprived of their natural shrimp food. Black, brown and grey colours are produced by melanins formed from amino-acids and appear as granules, with the intensity of the colour depending on the size and density of the granules.

Structural coloration is generally caused by a thin layer of many-sided cells, overlain by a transparent cuticle. If the cells reflect all light, the feathers appear white. Inside the cells of feathers that appear blue, green or violet are tiny, almost submicroscopic particles, or bubbles, that reflect blue or violet light. If the cells reflect blue light, the colour we see is blue provided the cuticle is clear; if the cuticle contains transparent yellow pigments, the reflected blue light appears as green. In most cases, a layer of melanin pigment below the

THE BIRDWATCHER'S NOTEBOOK

cells absorbs all the unreflected light, thus enhancing the blue or green colour.

Iridescent colours are caused by a variety of means involving interference to light rays. The most brilliant iridescence results from the submicroscopic light-reflecting particles being ordered into layers, about one blue or violet wavelength apart.

Basically, it is the body shape determined by the contours of the feathers and the colours that the feathers display, that enable us to identify birds.

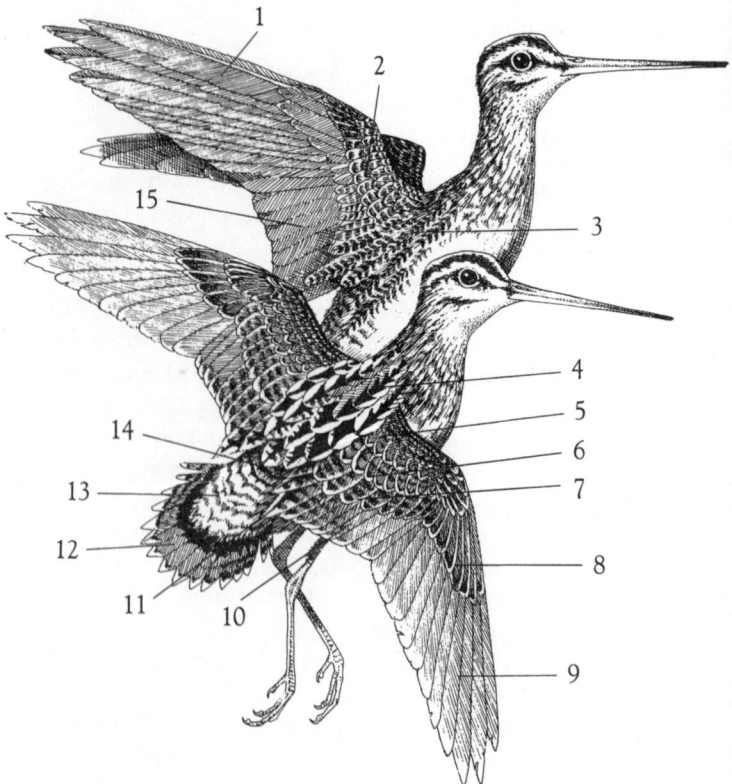

Fig. 4

Feather tracts of flying birds (Latham's Snipe): 1 primaries, 2 underwing coverts, 3 axillaries, 4 scapulars, 5 lesser coverts, 6 median coverts, 7 greater coverts, 8 primary coverts, 9 primaries, 10 secondaries, 11 tertiaries, 12 tail, 13 upper-tail coverts, 14 rump, 15 secondaries.

OPTICAL AIDS

Birds can be watched and appreciated with the naked eye, but a pair of binoculars adds so much to one's enjoyment that they ought to be regarded as essential. Binoculars are better for general use than telescopes. Telescopes, however, come into their own in places that are good for sedentary birdwatching, such as mudflats, estuaries and seashores, where waders and seabirds congregate, or for watching a nest at a distance.

BINOCULARS

Even a poor pair of binoculars is better than none at all. The first pair I tried, lent to me by a school friend, magnifying about 3× and with only one eyepiece operative, revealed a new world that has never since failed to excite me. However, to get the best use from them, one should invest in the best pair that can be afforded.

The first thing to do after purchasing a new pair of binoculars, particularly if they are your first, is to practise focusing and lining up on an object at different distances. It is much better to become familiar with their use in your backyard than to wait until you are on a birdwatching expedition. Most binoculars have two focusing aids, a large knurled wheel in the centre for most uses and a knurled ring on (usually) the right eyepiece, marked in dioptres, designed to synchronise the focusing of both eyepieces.

Many people have eyes of unequal acuity, to which they have learnt to adapt in everyday life, but when looking through binoculars this inequality is much exaggerated, so that one side focuses closer than the other, resulting in a fuzzy overall image. To overcome this discrepancy, the dioptre ring on the right eyepiece is used to match both eyes.

Line up on a clearly defined object, such as a car number plate, close the right eye and focus for the left eye with the central focusing ring. When the image is as sharp as you can get it, close the left eye and focus for the right eye with the dioptre ring on the right eyepiece. When this image is at its sharpest, open the left eye and the image should now be matched, sharp and clear. There is a scale on the dioptre ring; check it and remember the setting, for this will give you your optimum image. Thereafter, focus only with the central knob. If you wear your binoculars around your neck, you may find that friction causes the right-hand eyepiece to revolve slightly — a quick check every now and then that it is still set on the position you noted on the scale will ensure that you do not miss that fleeting glimpse due to having to readjust the focus.

If you are a beginner, you should, after matching your eyepieces, practise focusing on objects at varying distances. At first choose things that are easy to locate, such as TV aerials, street signs, house windows and so on. Alternate between close and distant subjects, so that you learn how to alter the focusing quickly. Soon you should be able to line up and focus immediately on any large object. Then set yourself harder tests, such as picking out a particular flower in a flower bed, or a leaf in a tree. It does not take long to become proficient, and so avoid a common deficiency among novice birdwatchers, vainly endeavouring to capture a clearly visible bird in the binoculars' field of view. When purchasing a new pair, you may find that they 'throw' left or right, high or low compared to the old pair, so you should practise until finding the new line becomes automatic.

Holding binoculars

The main problem in using binoculars is to hold them steady — the more powerful the magnification, the more difficult steadiness becomes. Some observers solve the problem by bracing their thumbs against the temples, others tuck their elbows into their sides, which is probably the preferred position. Where possible, it is a good idea to lean back against a tree or other solid support. At birdwatching localities involving large groups of birds, such as seashore, mudflats, breeding colonies and so on, a tripod is very handy. Camera stores stock several makes of clamp which enable binoculars to be mounted on a tripod. Ideally, a tripod should be light but sturdy, able to be extended to your full height, so that you do not need to stoop, and also able to collapse to a comfortable height when you sit on the ground. When used with a camera, a tripod usually has a heavy head but this is not necessary for binoculars and a simple light head is sufficient. A good model, which can be used as a yardstick, is the Slik SL67. With a telescope, such a tripod is essential.

For birdwatching from a car, one suggestion is to use an Eric Hosking invention, the rice bag. This is a small cloth bag, packed with rice and laid on a half-open window. The rice, if packed to the right density, enables the bag to rest on the glass edge providing sufficient stability to support binoculars (or a camera). The window can be wound up or down to give the most comfortable viewing position. Clamps are commercially available, but they are very expensive and are no better than the rice bag.

Cleaning binoculars

Great care should be taken when cleaning binoculars — spit and the tail of a shirt or handkerchief will degrade the finest optics to bottleglass. Before cleaning lenses, they should be thoroughly dusted with a brush and/or blast of compressed air (e.g. from a can of Blast Off, available from art or photographic stores). Then, with lens-cleaning tissue and lens-cleaning fluid, *gently* remove any smears. Cleaning of lenses should only be undertaken when necessary, not as a matter of course. Under no circumstances should you attempt to clean inside — leave this to a technician.

For wearers of spectacles

Nothing is more frustrating than having to take off glasses in order to use binoculars. The problem is caused by the protective flange around the viewing lens — if it is too deep, wearers of spectacles find that the field of view is vignetted. Fortunately, some models are suitable for use while wearing spectacles; they are designated as having 'long eye-relief', indicating that it is not necessary to have the eyes close to the lens in order to gain a full field of view. The wide-angle models also have a larger than usual viewing lens, which, coupled with a shallow flange, affords a full field of view. Most good modern designs, for example, Zeiss and Nikon, have rubber flanges on the viewing lenses that can be peeled back, allowing a full field of view and cushioning the spectacles from scratching.

Another problem associated with wearing spectacles is caused by peripheral light. When using binoculars without spectacles, the skin around the eye virtually touches the eyepiece, so most of the light reaching the eye is coming through the lenses. With spectacles, however, the eye cannot approach the eyepiece so closely and a large percentage of the light falling on the eye comes from outside the binoculars, which tends to degrade the image. Many people cup their hands to eliminate the extraneous light, but in this position the binoculars cannot be held as steady as usual. A possible solution is to cut a triangular piece of black cardboard and thread it over the spectacle wing, shaping it to fit against the cheekbone and temple, cutting out a lot of light. However, it also eliminates some peripheral vision while walking, so some experimentation may be necessary to cut a design that can be pushed back towards the ears when not needed.

Another factor worth considering is that most spectacles are ground to give optimum sharpness at about 5–10 metres as a compromise between distant and close viewing. When looking through binoculars or cameras this effect is exaggerated and, with some eye deficiencies, pin-sharp focusing is not possible as a consequence. Having my spectacles ground for infinity has greatly increased the sharpness of the image in my binoculars, which more than compensates for the corresponding loss of close vision in normal viewing.

How should binoculars be worn?

Most people wear binoculars around the neck but usually the strap provided is too long, so I suggest shortening it to the point where it just fits over your head. This will position the binoculars high up on the chest, minimising jolting while being in a handy position for use. Try the length with a piece of cord before you cut the leather strap. Carrying binoculars under the arm, with the shortened strap over the same shoulder, eliminates jolting altogether, particularly when climbing through fences and so on. It also protects them from rain. Some binoculars are very expensive and their owners, justifiably, feel obliged to care for them, so, if you prefer, carry them in their case, either with the strap diagonally over the shoulder or attached to a belt. However, binoculars are designed to be worn and, provided that they are kept dry, free from dust and are cleaned with great care, there is not much advantage in keeping them in their case while out birdwatching.

Choice of binoculars

To decide which pair best suits the individual, a number of points in addition to optical quality need to be considered.

Size and weight Towards the end of a long day in the field, the weight of heavy binoculars around the neck can be oppressive, and you wonder while staggering home whether a lighter pair might not be more sensible. Two of the most popular sizes, 7 × 50 and 10 × 50 are also among the heaviest. What are the virtues of these sizes and are they really necessary?

To answer these questions, you need to know what the sizes mean. Each pair of binoculars bears a designation consisting of two figures, for example, 6 × 30, 7 × 35, 7 × 50, 8 × 30, 10 × 50 and so on. The first figure indicates the magnification, so a 7 × 35 and a 7 × 50 give exactly the same magnification (seven times), even though the latter is double the weight and size of the former. The second figure indicates the diameter in millimetres of the large front lens (objective lens). It gives a rough indication of:

1. the field of view (how much you can see);
2. the amount of light gathered by the lens (how bright the image is).

So, the greater the number, the wider the field of view and the brighter the image, enabling better perception in lower light levels. Thus, in comparison with the 7 × 50, the 7 × 35 is not only smaller and lighter but has a narrower angle of view and a less brilliant image. In determining what is preferable, you must decide whether the saving in weight is worth the narrower, darker image. To obtain an estimated measurement of the light-gathering ability of a pair of binoculars, divide the larger number by the smaller, giving a figure known as the 'exit pupil', then square the result, for example, with the 7 × 50 the relative brightness (RB) is 51 (50 divided by 7 with the result squared); with the 7 × 35 the RB is 25. This measurement is an estimate because actual performance is affected by the coating of lenses, the quality of glass used and the optical design. An RB of about 15 or over is satisfactory.

A comparison of the RBs, weights and fields of view of different binoculars should be made before buying.

Magnification Most popular binoculars range between 6× and 16× magnification. It would seem that the most powerful would also be the most efficient. However, there are two disadvantages with really powerful binoculars.

1. The relative brightness is reduced, for example, 12×40 = 11.1 RB, 16×50 = 9.8 RB.
2. The greater magnification also magnifies any movement; it is very difficult to hold $12\times$ or $16\times$ steady enough for satisfactory viewing. A tripod is required, in which case one might just as well use a telescope.

The choice of a suitable magnification, therefore, depends on one's steadiness of hand; the choice will be determined by the most powerful magnification that can be held steady. Usually, beginners are most comfortable with $7\times$ or $8\times$, but, with experience, at least some come to favour $10\times$.

Focusing mechanism There are four types of focusing aid —
1. Individual focusing, usually indicated by the letters IF. In these models, each eyepiece has to be focused independently, enabling a more waterproof seal to be maintained. They are intended for use at sea or in the humid tropics

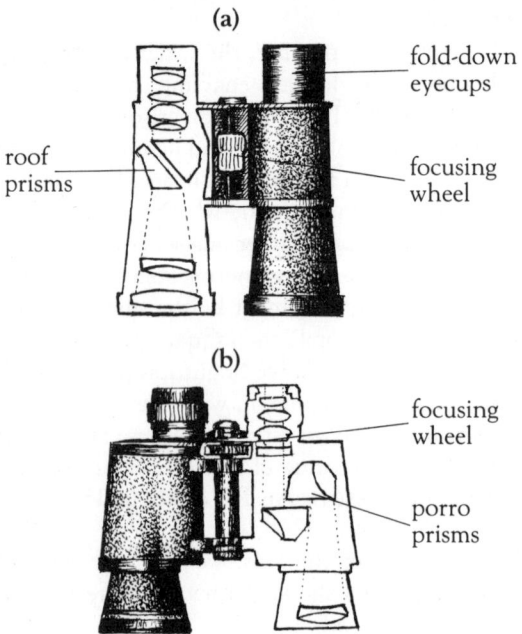

Fig. 5
(a) Roof (dach) prism binoculars; (b) traditional (porro) prism binoculars.

Pheasant Coucal: imagine this bird with teeth and you would have a fairly good idea of what an archaeopteryx looked like.

Raoul Slater

Male Tawny Frogmouth brooding its chicks during the day. Frogmouths are very variable in colour, although most adult males look like this.

Raoul Slater

and are *not* recommended for birdwatching. When buying a pair of binoculars, make sure they are not IF.

2. Central focusing, often indicated by the letters CF. A small knurled wheel moves both eyepieces as a unit when it is rotated. This is the commonest form of focusing. The wheel is placed so that it is operated with the index finger.

3. Zip or action focusing is a variant of central focusing, incorporating a much larger knurled wheel with a more positive response, resulting in quick changes to focus. The wheel is placed so that it is operated by the second and third fingers, which are not as manipulative as the index finger. It is rather more difficult to fine-tune the focus, so check if it suits you before buying. Tasco models call this 'zip' focusing, Nikon's terminology is 'action'. Another variant is a rocker mechanism in front of the wheel but I found this unsatisfactory during a brief test, since it required some tension to operate, resulting in some unsteadiness, but with persistence it could be satisfactory. The fact that this mechanism has not spread to other makes suggests that it is not popular.

4. Internal focusing on some roof prism models is a more sophisticated design, resulting in a more dustproof seal.

Close focusing Most binoculars do not focus closely enough for viewing small birds in nearby bushes. Some adjustments can be made because many brands focus 'beyond infinity', allowing washers to be added, and, therefore, some gains at the close end. This should be done by a repair technician. Some brands have a screw preventing the lenses from coming right off that can be adjusted or removed (a practice *not* recommended by the maker and care must be taken not to screw the lenses too far, as they are easily broken if dropped). If your choice comes down to a few models that you cannot otherwise separate, choose the one that focuses closest.

Optical quality Apart from the factors already mentioned, the optical quality is of the utmost importance. Basically, one pays for quality — the better the lenses, the higher the price. So it makes sense to buy the best that one can afford. If the budget is limited, there are a number of things to watch for in less expensive pairs. Test them outside the shop and look at something like a flagpole against the light; if there are coloured ghost images of the pole, or if the pole appears bowed towards the edges of the image, then the optics are probably inferior. Comparative sharpness can be judged by looking at car number plates or street signs.

Adding up all of these factors to make a decision as to the best pair is no easy matter and any advice tends to be very subjective. If size is a consideration, 8 × 30 is probably best, and, because of its close focusing ability, the Zeiss Deltrintem 8 × 30 MC is a good choice. If wide field of view is desired, 8 × 40 wide angle and if light-gathering power is required, 7 × 50. If difficult terrain is encountered — water, ice, snow, dust — the Minolta Mariner 10 × 40 comes highly recommended; if price is no barrier and the hand is steady, Zeiss 10 × 40 or Leitz 10 × 40 B (or BA) may suit but if the hand is not so steady, then possibly the Nikon 8 × 40 DCF, Leitz 8 × 40 B (or BA) or Bushnell Elite 8 × 42 would be better.

From a survey of a number of friends who use binoculars frequently, I found a wide spectrum of makes and sizes, all with happy owners. Finally, if in doubt, go to a bird club outing and try out as many as possible.

Care of binoculars

One feature of most binoculars is the incorporation of prisms in the design. The function of the prisms is to bend the light back and forth between the large front (objective) lens and the small viewing (ocular) lens, substantially reducing the total length of the instrument and also ensuring that the image is viewed the correct way up. The focal length of 8× binoculars is about 300 millimetres, so without the prisms they would be a minimum of 300 millimetres in length — the incorporation of the prisms reduces the length by about half. A minor disadvantage of prisms in cheaper models is that they can become misaligned after a heavy knock, resulting in a 'double' image. This fault is best fixed by a mechanic, as there may be a number of fiddly 'shims' to adjust for correct alignment.

Apart from the difficulty of adjusting the shims (and the probability of losing them), by opening up binoculars, the chances of dirt, dust and humidity affecting the interior lenses is increased. Also, the focusing barrel is 'sealed' by a special lubricant that prevents the intrusion of dust and humidity. Any amateurish tinkering is likely to negate the effectiveness of the seal. It is worth mentioning that the lubricant may run if overheated due to being left in the sun for lengthy periods, solidifying later in the wrong place. In cold weather, it may become stiff. If either extreme causes problems, or if you feel grit while focusing, it is advisable to have the lubricant replaced. This is only likely to occur in cheaper models; better brands resolve these problems in various ways. Swarowski, for example, use epoxy resin to shockproof totally their interior glass, others protect them from shock with ribbed rubber outer casing. Leitz and Zeiss have internal focusing mechanisms in some models. Nevertheless, by treating even armoured binoculars as precision instruments, you will be repaid with a lifetime's enjoyment.

TELESCOPES

While binoculars are suitable for most birdwatching situations, telescopes are preferable wherever long-range viewing of relatively sedentary birds is undertaken. Ideal situations for telescopes are beaches, estuaries, intertidal mudflats, lakes, pools, swamps and sand spits, where waterbirds, waders and seabirds congregate. Telescopes are also ideal for studying nests from a distance and, particularly, colonial nesting birds, which should not under any circumstances be approached closely enough for them to rise from their eggs or young. The further away they can be viewed the better; and I would seriously doubt the integrity of anyone claiming to be a birdwatcher who knowingly approached within 100 metres of a nesting Little Tern.

Because of their increased magnification ($20\times$–$60\times$) and their much reduced field of view, telescopes cannot be used satisfactorily without a tripod. The Slik SL 67 is the sort of tripod to look at, being light, rigid and sufficiently extensible for comfortable viewing, either standing or sitting. When testing tripods, check how steady they are in windy conditions; make sure the tripod does not vibrate.

As with binoculars, one pays for quality in telescopes. By far the best among refractors is 'The Renaissance', with a resolution close to perfection, using interchangeable eyepieces ranging from $10\times$ to $265\times$, but it is very expensive and so beautifully crafted that it seems almost sacrilegious to take it into the field. A smaller field model, the Oracle 3", with interchangeable eyepieces from $10\times$ to $200\times$, is available from the makers of 'The Renaissance', but is still beyond the purses of most birdwatchers. Best among the catadioptric telescopes is the Questar 1300 mm field model, equally expensive, with inbuilt eyepieces.

Types of telescope

There are several basic types of telescope. In order of complexity, these are:

Refractive telescopes (or 'refractors')

1. The draw telescope is an old-fashioned, usually brass, instrument with a number of tubes of different diameters, collapsing into each other. In general, this is unsuitable for birdwatching.
2. The astronomical refractor is large and barrel-shaped, with high-powered eyepieces and not suitable for birdwatching.
3. Spotting scopes are made primarily for range shooters, but are equally suitable for birdwatching. In general, they magnify from 20× to 30× but some have more powerful eyepieces. Most incorporate prisms in the design to decrease the overall length and to revert the image so you do not see things upside down. They are either of fixed focal length (eyepieces can be changed for degrees of magnification) or zooms (where the magnification can be continuously altered with the one eyepiece). In general, zooms are not as good as the fixed lenses, falling off towards the higher magnifications. Most popular among birdwatchers in Britain and Europe, where telescopes are much more commonly used than in Australia, are the Optalyth 30 × 75 GA and Swarowski 30 × 75.

Reflective telescopes (mirror lenses or 'reflectors') The optical designs of the Gregory, Newtonian and Cassegrain reflectors incorporate two mirrors, as shown in the previous diagram; they are used in astronomy and are not suitable for birds. Two designers, Schmidt and Maksutov, independently, added a corrector lens to the optics of the Cassegrain, enhancing its performance. Modern catadioptric spotting scopes ('cats') incorporate either the Schmidt-Cassegrain design (Bausch and Lomb, Pentax and most Celestron) or the Maksutov-Cassegrain (Questar, Celestron C90). Zeiss, I believe, uses a design similar to the Gregory (two concave mirrors) rather than the concave-convex mirrors of the other two. They all require a prism in front of the eyepiece, or ocular, to convert the image to upright.

In general, reflectors are heavier and bulkier than the spotting refractors and are more likely to become misaligned unless handled with care. The Questar Field Model sets the standard among the larger 'cats' and the Zeiss 30 × 60 B among the smaller. The latter is armoured for added protection in the field. 'Cats' are better than refractors where higher magnifications are required. In comparing models, check that the secondary mirror does not cause a dead spot in the centre of the image and, before buying any telescope, read the article by Charles A. Bergman: 'Audubon's Guide to Spotting Scopes' in *Audubon* magazine, July 1986, pp. 95–109.

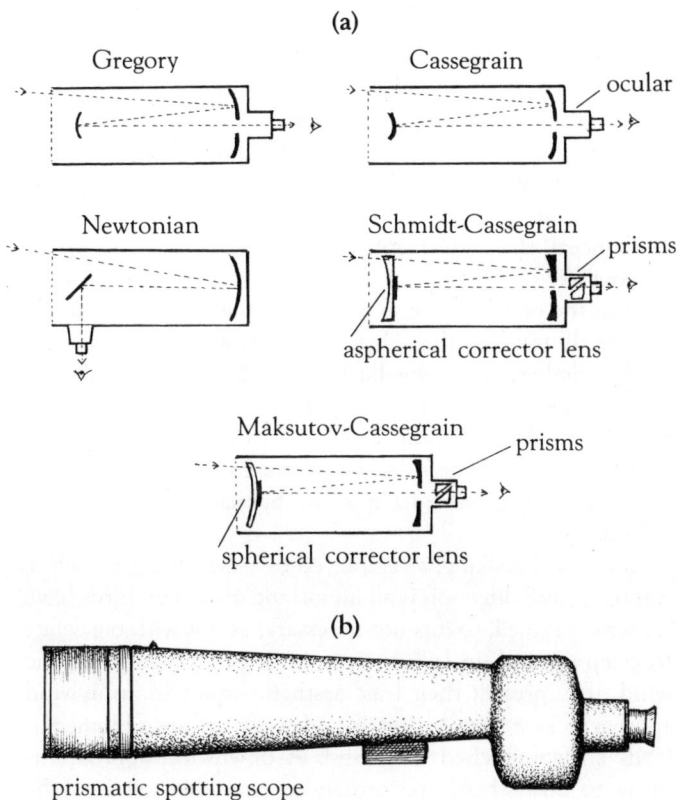

(a)

(b)

prismatic spotting scope

Fig. 6
Types of telescope: (a) reflectors; (b) refractor.

BIRDWATCHING TECHNIQUES

CLOTHING AND MOVEMENT

Much has been made of the need for camouflaged clothing for birdwatching. Stillness, however, is probably much more critical and, if coupled with inconspicuous, rather than camouflaged, clothing, is sufficient to view most birds. To break up the body outline, it is preferable to have upper clothing darker or lighter than lower.

When out in the bush with Wongaii Aborigines, I noticed how they could virtually disappear into the landscape by standing or squatting in the shade next to a bush or tree and maintaining utter stillness. I used the techniques they taught me for creeping up on wild kangaroos and, on one occasion, got to within 3 metres of a group of red kangaroos. Few birds are as wary as wild kangaroos, so it is possible to sneak up on most birds. The secrets, as explained to me by the Wongaiis, are:

1. Conceal the movement of legs and feet as much as possible.
2. If in the open, zig-zag so you are not at any stage moving directly towards the subject nor appearing to look at it.
3. If in timber, keep some bush or tree between yourself and the subject.
4. Move slowly, avoiding sticks and twigs that might snap.
5. If it looks as if the subject is about to leave, do not stop suddenly but ease to a stop. Similarly, do not start suddenly.

In classical stalking, as employed by gillies and great white hunters, wind direction is all-important. However, birds have no sense of smell, so it is not necessary, as it is with big game, to creep upwind. In fact, because birds perch facing into the wind, they present their least aesthetic aspect to an upwind approach. Best views, that is, sideways on are obtained if birds are approached crosswind. A downwind approach is likely to flush them prematurely as they take off into the wind, in other words towards the stalker, so they feel threatened sooner than they do if able to take off away from intrusion.

Unfortunately, there are some birds that cannot be approached closely, no matter how carefully one moves, for example, some birds of prey and waders. They have a 'ring of confidence' about them, an imaginary circle marking the closest one can approach without frightening them. Once this line is crossed, they are off. The Wedge-tailed Eagle probably has the largest ring of confidence of any bird. Some birds of prey, however, will follow humans through the bush, chasing grasshoppers or birds that are startled out. Occasionally, on regular routes, an association develops, enabling magnificent views — I have experienced such associations (with wild raptores) on a number of occasions with species including Brown Falcon, Collared Sparrowhawk, Little Falcon and Peregrine Falcon. The Peregrine Falcon, for example, followed me for a short portion of my daily route over a period of eight months and became extraordinarily tame. Although he chased hundreds of birds in that time, he never killed one, seeming to enjoy just harassing them; his favourite trick was to flip ducks over in flight. Such an association is something to be cherished and too easily abused to be shared.

Waders too are difficult to approach on mudflats as they usually occur where there is little cover. The colour of clothing here makes little difference. It is more productive just to sit comfortably and use a telescope. If you have to rely on binoculars, better wader-watching is obtained at places where one can get close, by moving up through mangroves or behind a bank, but the best is often at roosts where the birds congregate during high tide. By arriving at low tide and setting up comfortably behind whatever cover is available or by erecting a hide, you merely have to wait for the water to rise. It is a magnificent experience to have hundreds or thousands of birds densely packed only metres away. To be fair to such birds, either wait until the tide recedes and they leave or have an exit route that does not necessitate disturbing the roost. Arrive with plenty of insect repellent, for the stay could be a long one. Wader-watchers generally congregate where it is most convenient to view large number of waders — check with local bird groups for directions to such spots.

Apart from these few exceptions, most birds can be approached closely enough for satisfactory viewing with binoculars. For most beginners, however, it is more difficult to find the birds in the first place. There are always some that can be easily seen, common species such as Magpies, kooka-burras, Magpie-larks, cuckoo-shrikes and so on, but, while they may be very interesting birds, there is obviously more to birdwatching that just looking at these species.

SOME HINTS FOR BEGINNERS

Time of day More birds are active early in the morning than at any other time, so the best time for birdwatching is a period of two to three hours after sunrise.

Location Some patches of bush are better than others, a fact that can only be learnt by experience. Different birds inhabit different types of bush, so some research may be necessary if you wish to track down a particular bird. John Bransbury's book *Where to Find Birds in Australia* (Century Hutchinson, 1988) is very helpful.

Sound Often the best indication of a bird's presence is a call or song. To locate the direction of the call, try using both ears, moving the head slightly to the left or right until it appears that the song is directly ahead. Distance is harder to judge, being influenced by wind, calls from cicadas and by the quality of the song itself — making some calls seem closer than they are (e.g. cuckoos) and some farther away (e.g. Brown Thornbill.) Some birds, too, are ventriloquial and, therefore, very hard to pinpoint, for example, Crested Bellbird. It is often difficult to gauge the height from which the call is being made, but with growing experience it becomes easier to trisect direction, distance and height to give a rough indication as to where the bird might be. Raise the binoculars to just below the eyes, then watch for movement, trying to take in as much as possible of the area where you believe the bird to be. When a movement is detected, raise the binoculars to the eyes — now is the time to appreciate the practice in the backyard. If you cannot locate the bird, revert to the naked eye — searching around through binocu-lars is usually non-productive.

Movement Watching for movement is the name of the game and is really the hardest aspect of birdwatching to master. The good birdwatchers register the twitch of a tail, the flirt of a wing, the flick of a beak. Such fine-tuning of vision can be learnt, but only by experience. It is a bit disheartening being with a group, unable to see anything, when one person says 'There they are', another says, 'Thornbills', a third adds, 'Three Striateds and a Brown', and a fourth nonchalantly suggests 'All juveniles except for one of the Striateds', while you are still looking for the birds, pondering on the degree of experience represented among the others in the group. Take heart from the knowledge that even the best observers miss some birds and that the one who never makes a mistake is the one who says nothing.

Attracting birds

There are ways of making birds come to you. The simplest method is to 'squeak' through pursed lips, 'kiss' the back of the hand. This will attract many small birds. More sophisticated are 'squeakers', which are wooden gadgets that make a loud squeaking sound when rotated (available from the Bird Observers' Club). A small bottle of water with a cork is a cheap alternative; wet the cork, then rub it on the glass. As well as shivers up the spine, it will produce thornbills, warblers, wrens and others. Another alternative being used increasingly is a tape recorder. Even a poor recording will attract birds of the same species, particularly during the breeding season. I personally do not favour the employment of recorders, because of the disruption to nesting birds if used indiscriminately, but mainly because it makes it too easy to see certain difficult birds, negating the challenge, although I certainly do not begrudge their use to anyone else.

Banded Honeyeater

Joining a group

Beginners to birdwatching will learn much by joining a group, preferably one with not too many members. The best group to accompany is one where the members will encourage *you* to attempt an identification, rather than 'helping' you by just calling out the names of birds as they flit across your sight. For that reason, it is wise not to pretend to greater expertise than you possess — most birdwatchers are only too happy to assist a beginner. In particular, pay attention to calls and once again, if possible, try to put a name to a call rather than waiting for someone to tell you what it is. Don't be dismayed if you get it wrong or forget the call almost immediately — you will develop the ability.

One suggestion when in groups is to agree on a system of pointing out birds. Often one person spots a bird, then attempts to show the others where it is. 'Over there' with a vague wave of the hand is never much use. Think in terms of direction, distance and height, for example 'Beyond that black-barked wattle, 30 metres away in the white-barked eucalypt, about 15 metres up on diagonal branch'. Another method identifies the tree the bird is in, then imposes an imaginary clockface on the foliage: 'Third eucalypt, the one with hanging bark, about 2 o'clock, halfway to outer edge'. Establish beforehand whether the 'clock' encompasses the whole tree or just the leafy crown.

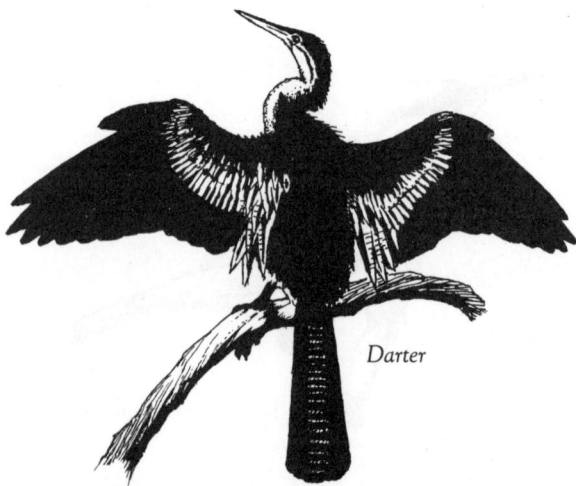

Darter

Expected behaviour in the field

The primary feature of civilisation is the imposition of controls on behaviour, basically determined by common sense and aimed at enabling us to live together without conflict. There is often a feeling that, once away from cities and towns, the need for considered behaviour is lessened, but the 'bush', while benign in most circumstances, can suddenly become a tyrant if common sense is abused. The first imperative is to leave the bush as you found it.

Fire Probably this is the most important consideration. I prefer not to make campfires, carrying a small stove instead, and I would strongly urge others to do likewise. Unfortunately, there is an equally strong urge among many to 'boil the billy' as part of the whole mystique of the bush, so if you must build a fire, at least do it correctly. In national parks, fireplaces are provided, so do use them. Away from parks, one can do no better than to follow the Boy Scouts' system, namely to clear a large circle around the fireplace, build a small fire with short pieces of wood, gathered from fallen timber or, preferably, with wood brought from home. When finished, extinguish with water and cover with dirt. Do not make a fire at all in windy weather or in periods of high fire danger. A gas stove on the tailgate of a car circumvents all potential problems.

Private property Much of the bush is on private property and permission from the owner should be obtained before venturing on to it. It is most thoughtless to consider making fires on private property, unless the property owner volunteers permission for you to do so. Generally, property owners are proud to think that there are birds on their land in sufficient numbers to attract genuine birdwatchers and they will usually offer any assistance. If their consideration has been abused in the past, and you are refused entry, respect their refusal and redouble your efforts to ensure that you do not engender similar dissatisfaction on your own field trips. Apart from lighting fires, landowners are particularly incensed by rubbish and litter, damage to fences, gates left open, disturbing stock and washing with soap, shampoo or detergent in troughs and waterholes.

Rubbish A constant source of annoyance in the bush is caused by rubbish left behind. Glass is the worst form of litter

— not only can it cause injury, but given the right circumstances, it can start a fire. Make it a rule to carry away any rubbish or, if you are in the bush for extended periods, to bury it. Tins should be 'burnt, bashed and buried'.

Personal safety Apart from the commonsense course of carrying a first-aid kit, there are a number of ways of ensuring personal safety. Few birdwatchers seem to get lost, but it is wise to let someone know where you are going and when you expect to return, just in case. It is easy to become temporarily disoriented in rainforest, sclerophyll forest and, surprisingly, in mallee or mulga scrub. In rainforest, it is wise, particularly for beginners, to keep to tracks and, if you need to move off the track to follow a particular bird, leave someone on the track to guide you back.

After some experience and as the terrain becomes familiar, you can expand your explorations, but, in general, unless searching for nests, the birdwatching along paths and tracks is just as good as it is deep in the forest; in fact, many species prefer the thicker cover where tracks allow extra light through the canopy. In mulga or mallee, it is necessary to walk much further to see a reasonable number of birds, so it is not difficult to lose contact. It is advisable to keep within 100 metres of a road or track, walking parallel to it, then crossing to the other side to walk back. If a good area or nest is found that warrants further study, walk directly to the road and leave a mark pointing to the spot, and time can be saved by tying a coloured plastic marker to a nearby bush. Don't forget to take the marker when you leave.

The following advice from Reg Johnson of the Bird Observers' Club of Australia, is worth heeding:

> Assuming that you do not expect to get lost, and have no survival equipment with you, there are still many things you can do to help yourself. To me, the most important thing is to have a safety line. This may be a road, a track, a prominent ridge or an edge of the bush. Then you can walk at right angles to intersect your safety line. A creek or river may have a bend, which causes you to walk further, but it will not go away.
>
> Make it a practice, when you are on a walk, to note where the sun is in relation to your track as you go out, or when the wind is blowing on your face. Be particularly careful to note when you cross a ridge or any watercourse, however minor —

to walk to 'safety' down the wrong gully can lead you further away. As you walk out, be sure to look back occasionally, because any country looks very different from the other direction.

The next most important thing if you become lost is to realise that you are lost as early as possible, then sit down, calm down and think. Do not waste energy purposelessly. If sitting and thinking gives you any idea of the direction in which to walk out, it is, in my opinion, safe to try it for an estimated period; if you are still lost after that time, do not continue.

If you decide that you definitely are lost:

- Stay put, preferably in a cleared area where you would be visible to searchers.
- At night make camp well before darkness.
- Find a natural shelter and improve on it if you can.
- Gather leaves and litter to make a bed to keep yourself off the cold ground.
- If you are lucky enough to have matches or powerful spectacles, you can make a small fire or two — big fires use too much wood, which must be gathered before dark.
- There is always some dry kindling in crevices and under logs. Bark and dry wood can also be whittled finely for kindling if you have a knife or blade. Remember that standing dead twigs are always drier than those on the ground.
- Should you have a fire, make smoke by day with green leaves to attract attention.
- Be careful to choose a place clear of litter for your fire. The Country Fire Authority will certainly find you, dead or alive, if you start a bushfire.
- Keep as warm as possible. To keep your head warm, you may have to be prepared for some other part of you to be cold.
- Should you be able to determine direction from the Southern Cross at night, be sure to use sticks and stones to mark the direction. If you do not, it will be hard to recognise by day.
- If you try to walk out, avoid walking in circles by selecting a continuous line of targets, continually choosing a new aiming point to extend your straight line.
- Chew on tender shoots, wattle gum or anything that tastes nice — it may not do you much good, but it keeps your spirits up.
- Liquid loss will be a major problem, so if you cannot find water, sop up the morning dew with a rag and suck it. If you

have nothing else, sacrifice your underwear for this purpose. Above all, keep calm and as warm as you can. Do not panic, but look after yourself until someone comes to find you.

Mr Johnson's advice is reinforced by that of Julia Huxley, Editor of the *Bird Observer*.

It is, of course, preferable not to become lost — don't forget:
- Do not wander off alone, especially in unfamiliar country.
- Study a map, check your bearings, weather, time and so on, and tell someone else where you are going and for how long you intend to be away, especially if, for some reason, you must go alone.
- If you are walking in the bush, be prepared. At the very least, wear sensible clothes and footwear, carry some food and water, matches, knife, torch and first-aid equipment. These items are easy to carry in a small day pack and you may be glad of them. Boy Scouts are encourage to take a compass and to carry a whistle to blow if they do become lost.

Laughing Gull

USING A FIELD GUIDE

Next to a pair of binoculars or a telescope, the most valuable tool for the birdwatcher is a field guide.

Minimum expectations of a field guide are:
1. It should be portable.
2. It should contain illustrations, text and distributions of *all* the species you could expect to find in the area it covers.
3. The illustrations should be arranged to enable easy comparisons to be made between similar species and should show all colour and plumage phases of each species likely to be seen. Each individual illustration should be clearly labelled to minimise crosschecking.
4. The text should give a concise description of each species, concentrating on those that can be most easily misidentified.
5. The maps should give a reasonably accurate idea of which species occur where.

Descriptions of calls

The least satisfactory component of a field guide is the descriptions of calls and songs. It is very difficult to transpose sounds into words and symbols. Usually the description only becomes meaningful once the song is known, by which time it is too late to be useful for identification purposes. Many bird songs just cannot be described in words, for example, those of the Brown Thornbill and the Rufous Whistler. Others fit perfectly into verbalisations, such as 'rigby-dick' for the Striated Pardalote: black-headed form, or 'dick-dick-the-devil' for the Crested Bellbird.

Recordings are more suitable, but run into two major problems — quality of reproduction and methods of retrieval. The former is a technical and artistic problem, and can only be overcome by the degree of dedication of the recordists. The second is the more difficult problem when used as a method of identification, diminishing in importance as experience grows. A good birdwatcher can narrow down a new call to a small group of probabilities and usually to genus, so a search can be made through, say, cuckoo calls or thornbill songs. But someone with less experience may have to go through the entire repertoire of passerine calls, which could take hours.

Many birds have such a variety of calls that it is likely that one or more could be missing from the recording. So the value of tracking down and seeing the bird uttering a call is self-evident. A bird's call alerts you to the fact that it is there; if it is a new call, you need to work to find out what bird is making it. Only if you can't catch sight of the bird should you try to track it down via a recording. If you can manage to make a recording of it yourself, no matter how poor, there is a good chance someone will recognise it.

One way in which comprehensive bird tapes can help is in learning bird calls in advance. A good example is provided by the notes of rainforest pigeons; they are notoriously difficult birds to spot and pre-knowledge of their calls can help to locate them. The chances of seeing some of the pigeons calling is not great, so it is easier to learn them from a tape. Similarly, when going to a new area, some knowledge of the calls to be expected will not be wasted effort.

There are some fine tapes of local birds in small areas, for example, *Birds of Iron Range* by Swaby and Griffin (available from the Bird Observers' Club of Australia), which not only allows calls to be learnt beforehand but can also be used, on the spot, to entice birds otherwise difficult to find. A comprehensive list of such tapes can be obtained from the Bird Observers' Club. These tapes contain information that a written field guide cannot give satisfactorily.

Turning up the right page

One problem with field guides is that they have to pack so much information into such a small space,* that it becomes difficult for less experienced observers to turn up the right page quickly. There are two solutions to this problem. You can browse through the pages sufficiently often to register a 'feel' for the way bird groups are ordered (most bird books are arranged in a similar way, so once learnt it can be universally

---

* In *The Slater Field Guide to Australian Birds* (Rigby, 1986), our efforts to include as much information as possible in a portable volume resulted in the use of a small typeface. Some observers may find it convenient to use a fresnel screen, available from optometrists for a few dollars, which, when laid across the pages, acts as a magnifying glass.

Eastern Yellow Robins courtship feeding.

Variegated Wren, the most widespread of the fairy wrens,
occurs practically everywhere except in rainforest.

Raoul Slater

helpful). Alternatively, stick tabs to the key pages, so that you can turn quickly to the pages on seabirds, birds of prey, owls or honeyeaters. To make tabs you can use Impac self-adhesive labels no. R1225, sticking one edge to the appropriate page then doubling it back to stick on the reverse side of the page, leaving 1–2 centimetres protruding. This can either be written on or coloured according to a suitable key kept at the beginning of the book. If you use a coloured key, the tabs are better if kept as narrow as possible (about 1 centimetre).

IDENTIFICATION PROBLEMS

It is hard enough, at first, just to work out different species, but identification problems may be intensified by the number of birds that have variable plumage:

Sexual differences

Male birds are frequently more brightly coloured than females, but in some species females are the more colourful, for example, Painted Snipe, Eclectus Parrot, Button-quail. Generally, the parent that spends more time rearing the young is plainer in appearance.

Plumage sequences

Plumage sequences occur in many species, resulting in young

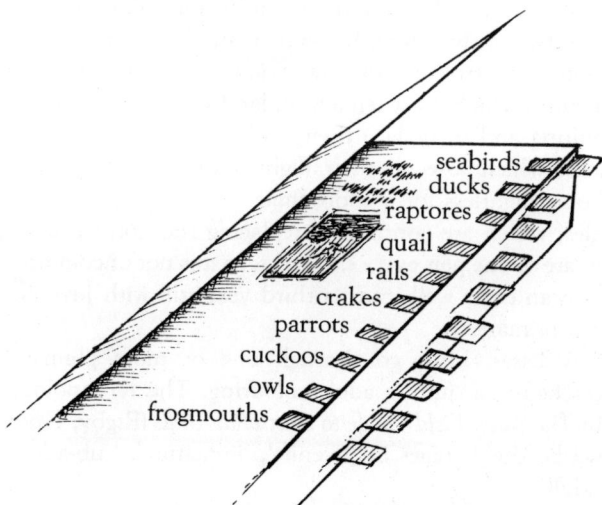

Fig. 7
Coloured tabs for quick reference.

birds that look quite different from adults. Feathers are surprisingly tough and can withstand a lot of wear, but inevitably they abrade and must be replaced by moulting. Generally, moult is periodic, occurring before the feathers become too worn. In some birds, changes to appearance occur as pale tips to feathers wear off — a classic example is the Common Starling, which in fresh plumage is heavily spotted but which becomes glossy black when the spots are worn away. In many birds, wear causes some changes to feather coloration; some become paler (e.g. Black Falcon), some brownish birds become greyish (e.g. Antarctic Petrel) and vice versa (e.g. Black-shouldered Kite). In terns, pale primaries actually become darker with wear. It is not possible to show all these variations in a field guide, but they should be kept in mind.

Most feathers can stand about one year's wear, so basic moults are annual, usually after the breeding season. However, many birds assume bright colours or ornamental feathers for the breeding season, so have two annual moults; the usual pattern is a body moult (that is, all but the wing and tail feathers) before breeding and a complete moult (including wing and tail feathers) after breeding. Exceptions are cisticolas and Franklin's Gull, which have a complete moult twice a year. Usually the moult is gradual, extending over one, two or three months, so that efficiency in flight and temperature control are not lost. Some exceptions are:

1. penguins, which must remain on land without food while moulting and so replace their feathers very rapidly;
2. ducks, which lose all their flight feathers at once and become flightless for a short time;
3. eagles, which are continually replacing their primaries at the rate of one pair every six weeks, so it is not uncommon to see an eagle well into its third year still with juvenile outer primaries.

In many cases, birds go through one or more plumage changes before acquiring adult colouring. The terminology used in *The Slater Field Guide to Australian Birds* (Rigby, 1986) to describe these stages is 'juvenile', 'immature', 'sub-adult' and 'adult'.

Not all birds go through all of these stages before achieving maturity, so it may be appropriate to look at some examples in ascending order of complexity.

1. Hall's Babbler: the juvenile is similar in plumage to the adult and once it has lost its yellow gape can hardly be distinguished from the adult.
2. Zebra Finch: the juvenile is similar to the adult female, but has a dark beak and eye. It has a body moult at 3–4 months, after which it looks like an adult and is capable of breeding.
3. Collared Sparrowhawk: the juvenile plumage is brown with coarsely streaked and barred underparts. It has a complete moult at the end of the first year into finely-barred adult plumage (the similar Brown Goshawk has two sub-adult plumages between juvenile and adult).
4. Eastern Yellow Robin: the juvenile plumage is streaked greyish brown. After several months the body feathers moult into adult-like plumage, but the juvenile wing and tail feathers are retained, so although it is virtually indistinguishable from an adult it is technically in immature plumage. At the end of the first year it moults completely into adult plumage.
5. Spotted Harrier: the juvenile plumage is reddish, often confused with Swamp Harrier, Red Goshawk and others. At the end of the first year, a complete moult results in mottled immature plumage. Another moult at the end of the second year results in adult plumage.
6. Wedge-tailed Eagle: the juvenile plumage is mainly brown. At the end of the first year it moults into a similar but darker immature plumage and repeats the process each year, becoming darker with each moult until, after 5–7 years, it is black. Because there is considerable variation between individuals, it is not possible to particularise these sub-adult plumages. Some individuals at six years are not dissimilar from juveniles, while others acquire a strikingly beautiful blond and black plumage at four years.
7. Splendid Wren: the juvenile is similar to the female but has a brown tail. After about six months, it has a body moult into immature plumage, acquiring female-like colouring; the tail is replaced more slowly, becoming blue at about eight months. At 10–11 months immature males moult into breeding plumage, then back again into brown (eclipse) plumage after the breeding season with a complete moult. In the second year, breeding plumage is acquired earlier than in the first year and is also worn

longer before going back into brown eclipse plumage. In subsequent years, the time spent in eclipse becomes less until, at 4–5 years, male plumage is worn all year.

8. Red-necked Stint: juveniles arrive in Australia in August–October from breeding grounds in the USSR and begin a body moult shortly afterwards into an immature plumage, which is like that of a non-breeding adult but with juvenile wings and tail. Another body moult in late autumn results in the sub-adult plumage, which is like the breeding adult but still with juvenile wings and tail (some birds stay in Australia over winter and do not moult into sub-adult). After the breeding season, there is a complete moult into non-breeding plumage. At the end of the second year adult breeding plumage is acquired after a body moult; the 'red' neck feathers have white tips, causing a strawberry look, but these tips wear off quickly, leaving bright chestnut.

There is still an enormous amount to be learnt about plumage sequences; any observer can contribute by systematic watching of even common birds, taking notes and publishing them in birdwatching journals. Advice on the best way to proceed may be obtained from bird clubs and from local bird-banders, who would probably welcome enthusiastic assistance.

Among the most difficult problems encountered by observers new to birdwatching are those due to birds moulting from one plumage to the next. They generally look tattered and motley, and resemble neither one plumage nor the other. Unfortunately, field guides cannot afford the space to show these birds, so, unless you enjoy a challenge, it is best to leave their identification until you are more experienced.

Geographical variations

Because Australia is such a large landmass with variable climate, there is a tendency for sedentary birds with wide distribution to vary in size or coloration. As a generalisation, one can apply several rules:

Bergmann's Rule As one moves north, birds of a particular species become smaller. This can occur gradually (e.g. Laughing Kookaburra), or in steps (e.g. White-throated Treecreeper), or in a single jump (e.g. Osprey). Where there is a clear contradiction of Bergmann's Rule one can suspect that the population involved may represent a distinct species. For example, many sedentary species in Tasmania are bigger than their mainland counterparts but some, such as the Australian Magpie and Southern Boobook, are substantially smaller, so may in fact be insular species. A bird of particular interest is the Australian Ground-Thrush. Until recently it was considered to be a local form of a species widely spread in Europe, White's Thrush. However, it has been shown that there are two species in Australia, one basically highland and one lowland. At this stage it is not clear which, if either, is more closely allied to White's Thrush, so it is better to keep them all separate. On the Atherton Tableland occurs a third, large form. It has been suggested that, because it contradicts Bergmann's Rule, it could be another species. In rebuttal, a corollary of Bergmann's Rule is cited, namely that birds become larger with increasing altitude. However, Atherton birds at 1300 metres are considerably larger than southern Queensland birds at the same altitude, so the argument continues and it is not inconceivable that there are three species of Ground-Thrush in Australia.

Geiger's Rule As one moves from humid to arid conditions, birds of a particular species become paler — good examples are Rufous Whistler, Black-faced Cuckoo-shrike and Grey Fantail. In the case of the Grey Fantail, the various populations, in general, follow Geiger's Rule, but in the mangroves in northern Australia where one would expect to find darker birds than in the interior, they are in fact paler and may represent a distinct species, Mangrove Fantail.

Evolution is a continuous process and various local factors that change over time, such as humidity, soil colour, prevalence of predators, density and background colour of vegetation and so on, may contribute to a population of birds changing in appearance.

In Australian birds we can see examples of evolution at work, particularly where populations of a species become isolated from each other. The degree of difference we can see in these examples is a reflection of the time that separation has been in effect:

1. no difference between populations — for example, eastern and western Elegant Parrots appear to be identical,

although widely separated;

2. slight differences not visible in the field — for example, Red-tailed Black-Cockatoo whose several populations differ only in minor measurements;

3. slight differences just visible in the field — for example, Little Kingfisher where the population in the Top End is more purplish than in Queensland;

4. visible differences, ranging from minor in eastern and western forms of White-naped Honeyeater (differing colour of bare skin over eye) to substantial, as in the rosellas.

If the differences are great enough, the forms involved are considered to be distinct species. Naturally, opinions differ as to which are valid species and which are not — some border-line cases are the Eastern and Western Yellow Robins, Hooded Parrot and Golden-shouldered Parrot, eastern and western forms of Little Wattlebird, Northern Rosella and Pale-headed Rosella, and the two forms of the Sooty Owl. There are many others. All make for fascinating arguments around the campfire. But, for the novice, it is quite confusing to find that two birds that are very similar, for example, the Atherton Scrubwren and the Large-billed Scrubwren, are different species, while two very different-looking birds, such as the Crimson and Yellow Rosellas, are the same species.

Some groups of birds are more difficult to identify than others because the differences between species are small. In most cases, the birds are dull in plumage with few patches of bright or contrasting colours. Most confusing are seabirds, waders, birds of prey and the small greyish or brownish bush birds known as thornbills and warblers (or gerygones).

With all of these groups, the best way to proceed is to build up familiarity with the commonest species. The better one knows the Sharp-tailed Sandpipers or the Wedge-tailed Shearwaters, the easier it is to detect birds that are different from them.

Seabirds

The difficulties of identifying the tube-nosed seabirds (petrels and shearwaters) are probably greater than those of any other group. In many cases they are seen from boats at a great distance. It is frustrating to see a bird a long way off over the waves and not be able to put a name to it. One has to be

Barau's Petrel

realistic — while there are a few observers who could have a good guess, it is just not possible to reliably name a bird so far away that any identifying features it may have are not visible. While there are some that can be immediately recognised, for example, some of the smaller petrels, the differences between many seabirds are often very fine, so a reasonably good view is necessary for a considered judgment.

In sorting out seabirds, the desirability of accompanying experienced observers is more important than it is with any other group of birds. With other birds, it is usually possible to move closer to get a better look at a bird about which you are uncertain. Binoculars or telescopes can be braced against a steady object, or mounted on a tripod for optimum viewing. In a boat, it is seldom possible to creep closer and the viewing platform is anything but stable. It is virtually impossible to use a telescope.

All of this means that the inexperienced observer has no way of verifying a tentative identification on the spot unless accompanied by more experienced companions. It is most valuable if the experienced members of the party allow the less experienced to attempt an identification. Rather than saying, 'No, it's a Providence', the experts should lead the novice: 'Did you check the underwing?', 'Is the head darker than the body?', 'Are the legs pale or dark?' If, having noted these identifying features, a name is still not forthcoming from memory, the beginner should then be encouraged to check the field guide. Hopefully, this should result in an identification. If not, the expert can then expound to his heart's content. In this way, the novice learns what features to look for — a sort of check-list: colour patterns, shape, width and angle of wings, shape and colour of bill, colour of legs, method of flight, whether communal or solitary.

Waders

When confronted with a vista of intertidal mudflats with perhaps thousands of birds, all brown or greyish-brown in colour, spread out picking for food, so far away that they show up as little dots in the binoculars, most novices wonder if they will ever be able to sort them out.

The seemingly insurmountable problem can be overcome by proceeding logically, moving step by step.

1. Light The task is made many times more difficult if one has to look into the light, so the primary consideration is to suit wader-watching to the best light conditions, that is, when the sun is behind your back. The coastline is convoluted, so that one can possibly find spots where good light conditions coincide with suitable tides. Generally, on the east coast of Australia, afternoons are best; on the west coast, mornings, and on the south coast, most daylight hours. At sewage treatment farms, salt works, small lakes and marshes, one can usually move around with the sun, so that viewing is possible at any time of the day.

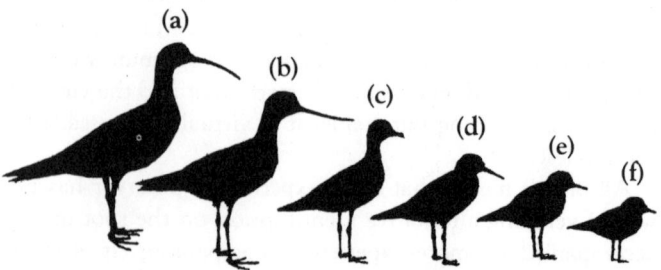

Fig. 8

Comparative sizes: (a) Whimbrel; (b) godwit; (c) Golden Plover; (d) Sharp-tailed Sandpiper; (e) Sanderling; (f) stint.

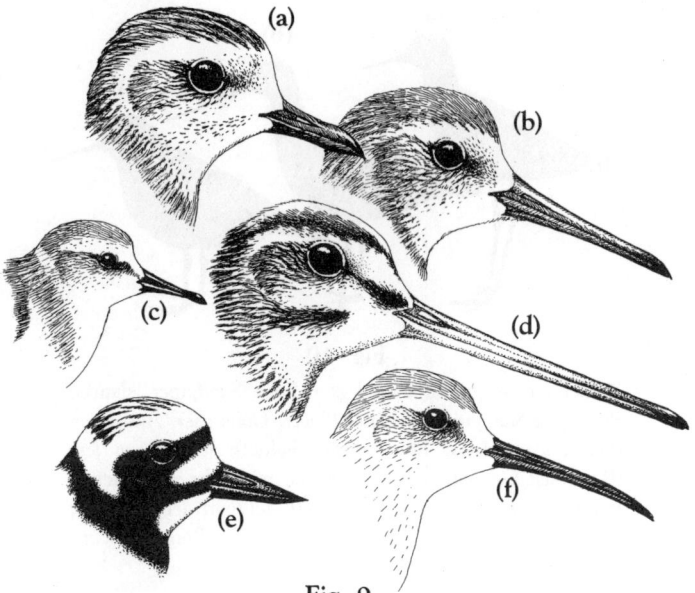

Fig. 9

*Wader bill shapes: (a) short and stout (plovers and dotterels);
(b) long and tapered (sandpipers); (c) short and slender, slightly
bulbous tip (stints); (d) very long (snipe, godwits, Dowitcher);
(e) short and chisel-like (Turnstone); (f) downcurved (Curlew
Sandpiper, Dunlin, Western Sandpiper, Cox's Sandpiper,
Broad-billed Sandpiper, Stilt Sandpiper, curlews, Whimbrel).*

2. Tides In coastal localities tides are all-important. Waders
spread out to feed during low tides and congregate at roosts
during high tides. Favoured roosts are sandbanks that remain
above water at highest tides, rocky outcrops, mangroves,
islands and marshes behind coastal dunes or behind mangroves. When tides begin to recede, waders leave the roosts
and follow the tides out, doing the majority of their feeding
at this time. Much less feeding occurs when the tide is coming
in, so optimum watching on intertidal flats is from just after
high tide to low tide. At roosts, best watching is as the tide
reaches its peak.

3. Size The first important key to identification of waders is
size, shown in Figure 8.

4. Bill shape First look at bill length. Plovers and dotterels
with short stubby bills are neatly separated from sandpipers,
snipe, godwits and tattlers with long slender bills (see Fig. 9).

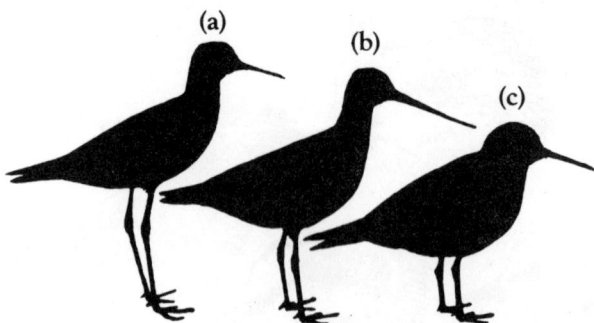

Fig. 10

Wader leg length: (a) long legs (Marsh Sandpiper, shanks, Ruff, Stilt Sandpiper, Oriental Plover, Dowitcher, Australian Pratincole, curlews, Black-tailed Godwit); (b) medium legs (Bar-tailed Godwit, most sandpipers, most plovers, Oriental Pratincole, all dotterels, Whimbrel); (c) short legs (tattlers, Dunlin, knots, stints, Turnstone, Sanderling, Ringed Plover).

5. Leg length See Figure 10.

6. Learn familiar species Learn the commonest species first — in their size categories, they are (see Fig. 8):

   (a) Curlew, Whimbrel
   (b) Bar-tailed Godwit
   (c) Greenshank, Golden Plover
   (d) Sharp-tailed Sandpiper, Curlew Sandpiper
   (e) Broad-billed Sanderling
   (f) Red-necked Stint, Red-capped Dotterel

Having sorted them out makes it easier to relate less common birds to them, for example, what is a bird the size of a Sharp-tailed Sandpiper with a similar bill but other, different features? Examination shows different eyebrow pattern, breast strongly marked with sharp cutoff and paler legs. Most probably it is a Pectoral Sandpiper. Check other possibilities but Cox's Sandpiper is ruled out as it has a slightly drooping bill and darker legs, and female Ruff can be eliminated because it has little marking on the breast.

Birds of prey

The main problem in identifying raptors is in gaining familiarity with them. While a few species are common and thus easily identified, for example, Kestrel, Black-shouldered Kite, Brown Falcon, Whistling Kite, Brahminy Kite, White-breasted Sea Eagle and Wedge-tailed Eagle, the others are less often observed and, even then, usually when soaring at some height. The second problem is caused by the number of juvenile and immature plumages that are sufficiently confusing to make confident identification difficult. But just as waders have their devotees, so raptores attract passionate adherents, able to pinpoint even the most confusing bird at incredible distances. They rely as much on the 'feel' of the bird as its field marks. In addition, they always seem to know when a bird of prey is approaching — a skill not as difficult as it seems, for they are listening for alarm calls, mainly from honeyeaters. Learn these notes and you too will be ready for that fleeting glimpse of a goshawk dashing by, or a more leisurely viewing of an eagle against the clouds.

To identify birds of prey in flight there are two things to watch for that may help.

Fig. 11

Different postures adopted by Black Kite during one minute's soaring, showing how variable a raptor can appear.

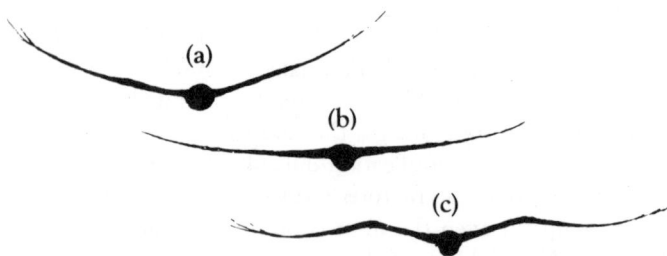

Fig. 12
Dihedral: (a) upswept; (b) flat; (c) bowed.

1. **Dihedral** This is the angle at which the wings are held while soaring. As dihedral aids stability in flight, it is more pronounced in slower species. It is particularly useful in separating some plumages that are often confused, for example, immature Black-breasted Buzzard with strong dihedral and dark phase Little Eagle with flat wings; Square-tailed Kite with pronounced 'V' and similar kites (e.g. Whistling, Black and juvenile Brahminy) all with flat or bowed wings; Brown Falcon and Red Goshawk from all other falcons and goshawks.

2. **Wing shape** Type of flight is reflected in the shape of the wings; fast flyers such as falcons have long pointed wings, but the wing changes to a more rounded shape in soaring. Birds that make a quick dash at quarry, such as sparrowhawks and goshawks, have short rounded wings. Soarers have long rounded or square-ended wings, usually showing prominent 'fingers' — eagles and kites usually show six fingers and harriers five. The Crested Hawk (or Pacific Baza) has unusual broad wings nipped in towards the body.

Small bush birds

Many small birds found in the bush are brownish, greyish brown or brownish grey, with distinguishing marks that require close observation to be seen. They are generally similar enough for many observers to lump them as 'LBJs' (or 'Little Brown Jobs') and give up without a fight.

There was a time when it was difficult to put names to some small bush birds because the concept of species was different then and many forms, which we now know constitute a single species, were regarded as two or more separate species. For example, at the beginning of the twentieth century, 19 species of thornbills were recognised, compared to the current 11. Judgment, in the past, as to which species was which was largely subjective and there was some justification for considering small bush birds difficult to identify. Even though our species concept is now more rational, the belief remains that the difficulties are almost insuperable. Rubbish!

The way to success, as with other groups mentioned, is to:

1. Familiarise yourself with common species — do this not only visually but, more importantly, through songs and calls. If you can recognise the calls of Brown Thornbill, Weebill, Brown Warbler, Buff-rumped Thornbill and White-browed Scrubwren, you are well on the way.

2. Eliminate impossibilities first, then improbabilities. You will then find the problem suddenly becomes much easier. This elimination is done in a number of ways.

    (a) *Distribution* — for example, if you are near Melbourne, you are not going to see an Atherton Scrubwren.

    (b) *Habitat* — if you are in woodland, you won't see man-

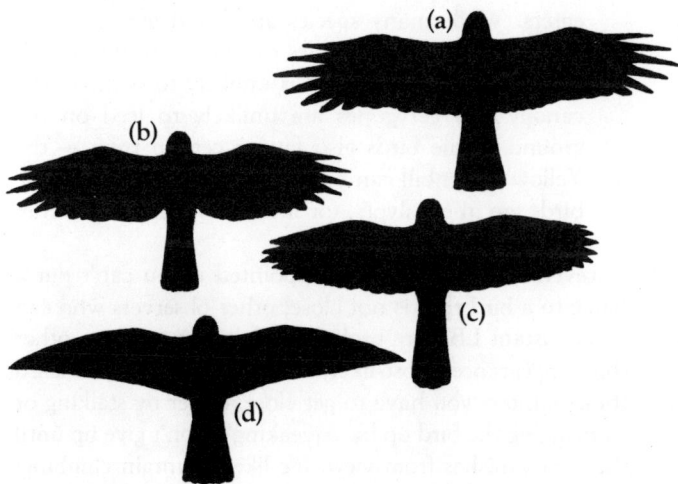

Fig. 13

Wing shape: (a) soarers have long square-ended wings with prominent fingers; (b) Bazas have nipped-in wings; (c) goshawks have rounded wings for pursuit through bushes, (d) falcons have long pointed wings for pursuit through open spaces.

grove species. For novices, a good way to begin is by marking up the field guide with a coloured marking pen. Simply put a mark on the colour plate over the name of any bird likely to occur in your area (make sure the ink in the marking pen is transparent and that it doesn't bleed through the page). If you make the mark small, room is left for other colours to be placed alongside to indicate likely birds in more distant localities.

(c) *Microhabitat* — within each broad habitat such as woodland, rainforest and so on, there are a number of microhabitats, ranging from the ground to the tree-top, each occupied by particular species. Some species spend much time on the ground, for example, Speckled Warbler, Pipit, Bushlark, Pilotbird, Logrunner and most scrubwrens. Some species occupy low, dense shrubbery, for example, fieldwrens, fairy-wrens and heathwrens. Grasses are occupied by some wrens, cisticolas, grassbirds and finches. The lower canopy harbours Brown Thornbill, Brown Warbler and in the upper canopy are found numerous honey-eaters. While many species are found across several microhabitats, some species can be safely eliminated, for example, the Pilotbird is unlikely to occur in the canopy and gerygones are unlikely to feed on the ground. Some birds also favour certain trees — the Yellow Thornbill can be fairly safely eliminated if the birds are in eucalypts, for it favours she-oaks, wattles and similar trees.

4. Perseverance — don't be disappointed if you can't put a name to a bird that is not close; other observers who can name distant LBJs are probably relying on pointers other than appearance, most likely the call. So, until you learn these pointers you have to get close, either by stalking or by bringing the bird up by 'squeaking'. Don't give up until the bird vanishes from view. It's like mountain climbing: you don't reach the summit by going downhill.

WHAT NEXT?

Once the observer is able to identify birds with reasonable certainty and accuracy, there comes a point when the desire for a new challenge arises. There are any number of ways that an interest in birds can be extended, ranging from solipsist (e.g. 'twitching') to co-operative (e.g. bird-banding). Some options are discussed on the following pages.

PHOTOGRAPHY

One of the most pleasant and satisfying ways of extending an interest in birds is through photography. There are several ways of approaching the subject.

Physically, one can either actively pursue birds by stalking, or passively sit and wait (usually by using hides at nests, waterholes, food sources or roosts). The equipment necessary is rather different for each method, and the results tend to exhibit different qualities.

Emotionally, one can approach the subject ornithologically, that is by making the bird more important than the picture, or artistically, by making the picture more important than the bird. Ideally, the best bird pictures blend ornithology and art, where bird and picture are of equal importance, but these are not common. Each sort of picture has its place, so the ornithological photographer need not aspire to artistry if it is alien to his nature, and vice versa.

Stalking birds with the camera

This could be defined as the art of benign hunting, causing neither death nor anguish to the quarry, resulting in trophies far more interesting than moulting heads on den walls. The main hurdle to overcome is getting close enough to the subject for an acceptable result. One of the commonest mistakes is trying to get too close, in other words, trying to 'fill the frame', but not getting consistently close enough is equally boring. The word 'consistently' is used advisedly because, in the terms of an individual's photography, variety adds interest. If, in each picture, the bird occupies the same position and dimension, the ultimate result is boring. So try to avoid taking pictures with a technical sameness about them.

As a benchmark, I think that pictures where the bird occupies about one-third to one-quarter of the picture area are the easiest to compose satisfactorily, and probably have greatest appeal. If the bird is much bigger, it dominates the space and one has to cope with the problem of the bird looking out of the picture rather than into it (the artist Robert Bateman can get away with it, but few others can). Probably the least aesthetic result of all is the shot with the bird's beak crammed into the top right-hand corner and the tail in the bottom left; it is only marginally worse, however, than the reverse — beak top left, tail bottom right. It is more pleasing to have the bird smaller than our one-third to one-quarter benchmark than to have it larger.

The second hurdle to overcome is to learn to look at the whole image on the ground-glass screen, not just at the bird. Try to avoid distracting elements such as out-of-focus highlights, broken branches and so on. The easiest option is to use the shallow depth of field inherent in telephoto lenses to blur out everything but the bird and its perch. This, too, quickly becomes boring unless other considerations such as lighting, colour and balance are employed sensitively. For this reason, most successful stalking shots are taken in low-light situations, particularly early morning and evening — the hour following sunrise and the hour before sunset are the most productive; not only is the light more mellow, but dra-

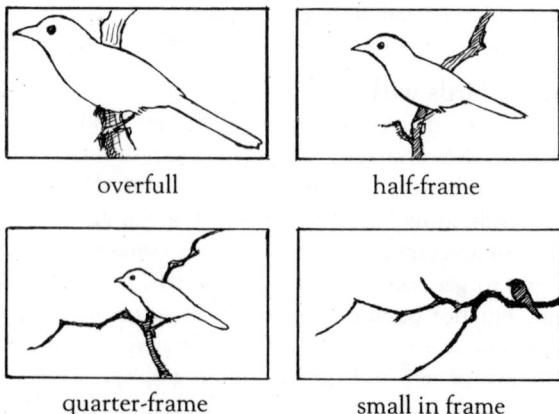

overfull   half-frame

quarter-frame   small in frame

Fig. 14
Picture area.

Male black-backed form of the Splendid Wren; females are greyish brown with a blue tail. A co-operative species, as many as five fully-coloured males have been seen attending one nest.

Raoul Slater

Spotted Bowerbird displaying to female. The lilac nape
feathers are usually kept hidden.

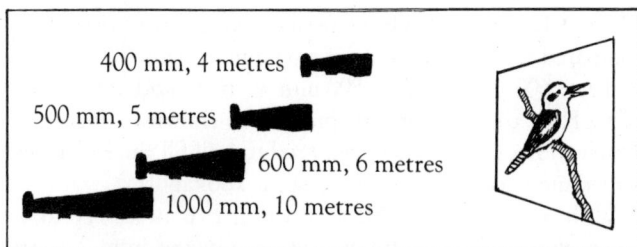

Fig. 15
Optimum focal length.

matic back-lighting effects are much easier to achieve. However, there is a serious drawback to taking pictures at such times: the light level is low and it may be necessary to use slow shutter speeds, so the failure rate is sometimes high. There are possible trade-offs:

1. You can use faster films, allowing faster shutter speeds, but you lose sharpness because such films are grainier. Grainy effects can be aesthetically satisfying, but only rarely. Particularly in books, grainy pictures often look out of place (but not always — see the lovely picture of a Striated Thornbill by R. Graves in *Wrens and Warblers of Australia* (Angus & Robertson, 1982).

2. You can use a lens with a wider aperture, allowing more light to reach the film, but such lenses are much heavier and are very, very expensive.

It is much more difficult to take a satisfactory picture that includes elements other than the bird and its perch, and considerably more knowledge of composition is required to take such a picture and to appreciate it.

Equipment for stalking As camera, lens and tripod have to be carried and manoeuvred through the bush, across mud-flats or among the mangroves, it can readily be appreciated that the largest telephoto lens is not necessarily the most satisfactory. Without going into optical details, there are two factors that influence weight — focal length and maximum aperture. The greater the focal length and/or the larger the aperture, the heavier the lens. The focal length (usually given in millimetres) determines how close it is necessary to approach a bird to get a reasonable shot. Some idea of focal length may be given by the degree of magnification. A

400 mm lens (the smallest useful stalking lens) enlarges 8×
compared to a normal lens on a 35 mm camera; 500 mm lens
= 10×; 600 mm = 12×; 800 mm = 16×; and 1000 mm =
20×. How this converts in practice is shown in Figure 15,
which shows the distances required to half fill the frame with
a medium-sized bird, in this case, a kookaburra.

With a small bird, such as a wren, it is necessary to get
much closer for a half-frame picture, ranging from 2 metres
with a 400 mm lens to 5 metres with the 1000 mm lens. To
do so requires a close-up tube to be mounted, in most cases,
between the lens and the camera, reducing the amount of
light falling on the film and so requiring an increase in
exposure. Most telephoto lenses do not focus closely enough
for a full range of images of small birds, so a close-up tube
is a handy accessory. Mirror lenses are better in this respect
than normal lenses.

In making the choice of the most suitable *lens*, it should
be mentioned that there are two basic types — the normal
straight lens and the mirror lens.

Mirror lenses have some advantages; they are more compact and generally lighter than comparable normal lenses and
they focus closer without accessory tubes. But they have four
disadvantages:

1. They are 'slower', that is, they have smaller apertures than
   normal lenses, thus requiring slower shutter speeds.
2. The aperture is fixed so the lens cannot be stopped down
   for increased depth of field.
3. Highlights in out-of-focus areas form 'doughnuts' that,
   while capable of being used creatively, in most cases are
   obtrusive.
4. They are often difficult to focus. The mirror lens is possibly more suited to photographers who just want nice pictures of birds or who wish to acquire a collection of as
   many species as possible, or for the artist who wants reference material. Within their limitations mirror lenses can
   produce beautiful results but, I feel, less consistently than
   normal lenses.

Choice of lens will also be dictated by the degree of your
commitment. This may require some soul-searching, but it is
futile to spend a lot of money on the best equipment if it is
not coupled with the strong desire to succeed or the sensi-
tivity to do it well. It may be worthwhile to do a 'dummy-

run' with some timber of the approximate size and weight of a camera on a tripod and see how you manage in creeping up on a variety of birds. It is not quite the same as using binoculars — a bird looks good through binoculars even at some distance. When translated via a camera lens on to film, a bird at the same distance doesn't look nearly as good.

If still convinced that stalking is the desired option, then a lens in the range of 400 mm to 600 mm in focal length is probably the most suitable. A fixed focal length rather than a zoom is usually better. The aperture chosen should be the largest that can be afforded; f6.3 is the cheapest, followed by f5.6 — anything larger than that, for example f4.5, f3.5 or f2.8 becomes staggeringly expensive, as well as very heavy. This is reflected in the current prices (in Australian dollars) of some 400 mm lenses:

Aperture	1988 price ($)
f6.8	1 160
	2 172
f5.6	498
	675
	1 086
	1 927
	3 170
f4.5	3 201
f3.5	8 112
f2.8	11 777

A realistic compromise is a 300 mm f4 lens with a 1.4× doubler (giving an effective 420 mm f5.6) or with a 2× doubler (600 mm f8). It is certainly neither a heavy nor a bulky combination, but depends very much on the quality of the doubler — the best cost as much as some lenses. A cheaper alternative is a 200 mm f2.8 lens with a quality 2× doubler, giving an effective 400 mm f5.6.

I began with a 400 mm f5.6 and have never regretted it, but

realise I would have managed a few more shots with a 600 mm while being more uncomfortable carrying it.

The *camera* is less of a problem if the lens is one made by one of the lens specialists such as Tamron, Vivitar, Sigma or Soligor. Almost any type of 35 mm single lens reflex (SLR) will do the job, preferably one with automatic as well as manual exposure control. Many of the innovations on modern cameras are not needed for stalking, so the top-of-the-range models are a waste of money. Something light and reliable, perhaps with a quiet motor drive, would be ideal. At the moment, probably the Contax 137 is as good as any, having the quietest motor drive and an exceptionally bright ground-glass screen.

If one of the very expensive lenses, such as Nikon or Canon, is the choice, it makes sense to buy a camera made for the lens. The most preferred option among professional wildlife photographers seems to be the Nixon FE2 with 600 mm f4.5, or the Canon F1 with 500 mm f4.5.

The *tripod* is just as important as the camera. It needs to be rock-steady and capable of extension well over your head so you can stand comfortably upright when the lens is pointed up. Such a tripod is, of necessity, heavy and probably weighs more than the optical equipment. To carry it, some relief may be obtained by attaching a cushion to the shoulder. Some photographers use 'gunstock' mounts instead of tripods but I am not convinced that they are satisfactory. If tempted to buy one, first compare pictures taken using the

Australian Shelduck

two pieces of equipment. Photographs taken with a camera mounted on a gunstock feature in *Inland Birds of Saudi Arabia* by J. Silsby (Immel Publications, 1980) and good examples of shots using tripods are found in *The Great Australian Birdfinder* by Michael Morcombe (Lansdowne, 1986).

To carry any additional equipment is verging on masochism, but several items may be of interest.

A *small tape recorder* is very handy for calling up birds into photographic range.

An *extender* or *'doubler'* can be added to the lens to increase its focal length without adding much weight. In general, doublers are not entirely satisfactory, as they severely decrease the amount of light falling on the film, requiring slower shutter speeds. They tend to degrade the image, leading to less sharp pictures and they cause the image on the ground glass to darken, making it harder to focus.

A *fresnel screen* can be used in conjunction with an electronic flash to throw light into dark situations. It is to the flash what the telephoto lens is to the camera. It is much more an implement for the ornithological photographer who wishes to record displays and feeding behaviour at night or in places like rainforests. A suitable fresnel screen can be bought from opticians, who sell them to people with poor eyesight, enabling them to enlarge the print in books and newspapers. It costs only a few dollars and measures about 20 × 25 centimetres. It consists of a sheet of plastic embossed with a series of fine circles that create the effect of a weak magnifying glass. Its great virtue for photographers is that it can concentrate the light from a flash into a beam, enabling it to be thrown a considerable distance. Optimum usage requires some testing to determine how far the screen should be held from the flash to throw the most suitable beam.

The simplest way is to mount a dedicated flash on top of the camera, then position the screen about halfway along the barrel of the lens at the appropriate distance determined by testing. To hold the screen rigid, some sort of support needs to be made from aluminium, capable of being clamped on to the lens. The screen needs to be centred by focusing on a white wall from 6 metres or so, then firing the flash manually while watching through the ground glass and making adjustments until the field of view is covered. The correct distance between screen and flash is determined in the same way. If the fresnel screen is positioned at exactly its focal length from the flash, a virtually parallel beam is created, but it shows an image of the flash tube, which results in uneven lighting, so it is best to position it just out of focus so the beam, while not parallel, lights the subject evenly. Correct exposure can be left to the camera if the flash is dedicated, but testing will be required if it is not. If you find this sort of accessory useful, it would probably pay to make a more permanent housing for the fresnel screen — a box made from taped foamboard and lined with aluminium foil is light and reasonably rigid.

Hide photography

The function of a hide is to shield the observer from the subject's view, enabling observations to be made at close range. It can be made of any material, from a few leafy branches to lofty aluminium and canvas towers. A simple, cheap and effective hide is a wool bale, which can be purchased from bag merchants for a few dollars. In colour, wool bales are pale beige, so a little camouflage can be added with olive and brown dyes or paint. Birds accept hides whether they are obvious or not; the function of the camouflage is to minimise attention from humans. Another invaluable item is a bale of binder twine, which should last for many years.

The hide at ground level There are two simple ways of putting up a hide on the ground:

1. Attach a length of binder twine to each corner and suspend from nearby trees or branches.

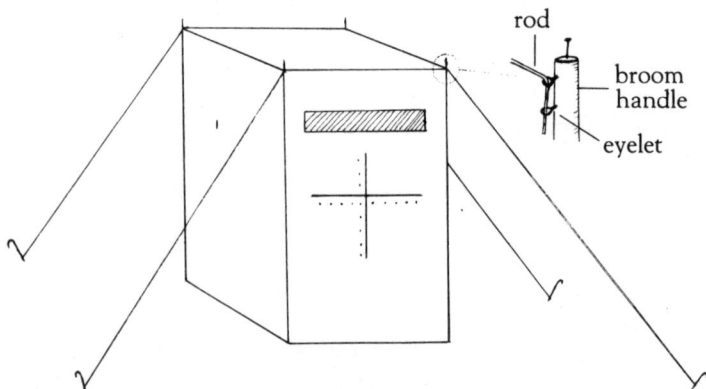

Fig. 16
Wool-bale hide.

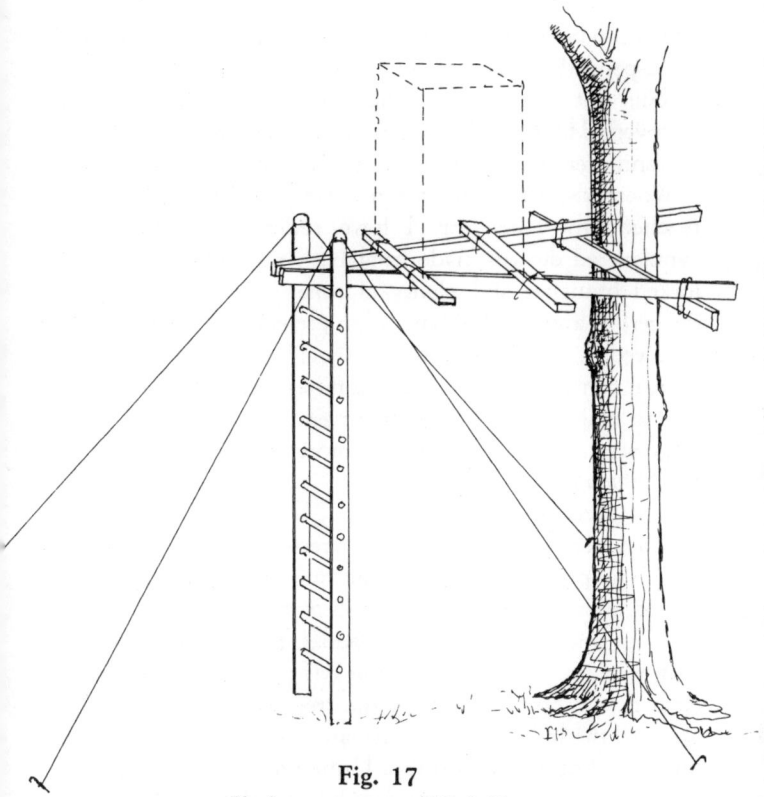

Fig. 17
Platform using extendible ladder.

2. Drive 1.5 metre stakes into the ground and drape the hide over them. Longer stakes can be used if hessian or other material is attached to the bottom of the wool bale to conceal the observer's legs.

The hide above the ground To use hides for observing birds at arboreal nests, it is necessary either to build a platform in the tree or to use a tower.

Usually it is a simple matter to tie lengths of timber between upright branches, forming a triangle to support a platform. A practical platform can be made from two lengths of 6-ply measuring about 175 × 75 centimetres joined together along the longer side by a pair of strong hinges. Rope handles attached to the sides opposite the hinges make it easier to carry and to haul up into the tree. Not all trees have convenient upright branches, but usually other arrange-

61

ments can be made. Some solutions that have been used are:
1. suspended by wire or rope;
2. built out from a large upright trunk with inverted forks;
3. inverted forks used between two slender upright branches;
4. cantilevered beyond an upright branch.

When wishing to observe a nesting bird that cannot be reached any other way I have resorted to all sorts of cantilevered devices made from bush timber and involving forked branches and plenty of rope. These are extremely dangerous and, while I have been prepared to take the risks involved, I cannot recommend them to anyone else. However, it can be said that, given sufficient incentive, it is possible to build a hide at any tree nest.

Towers are safer and usually more convenient, but have two disadvantages:
1. They are expensive.
2. They are heavy to transport, erect and manoeuvre.

The simplest and cheapest solution is the extendible ladder in conjunction with lengths of 75 × 50 millimetres timber. Use this system by guying the ladder in an upright position with four ropes near a tree, then tying two of the lengths of timber, one on each side of the tree trunk, and attaching them to the ladder. Crosspieces are then tied between these and the platform laid on top. Using an 8 metre ladder, any nest up to 9 metres off the ground is within reach.

A cheap tower can be made from galvanised water pipe. We use one constructed from sections, each consisting of two 3.5-metre lengths of pipe, joined by two 1.5-metre lengths. Two sections are joined together by 1.5-metre lengths attached by fencing couplings, then stood upright and guyed with ropes. A 30-centimetre piece of steel rod with a washer welded around the middle is dropped into the top of each upright pipe, allowing the next section to be added.

Safety on these towers depends on the guy ropes, so it is essential that they are maintained in good condition and replaced as soon as fraying becomes apparent. With this type of tower it is unwise to work at greater heights than 10–12 metres.

More expensive towers can be made from aluminium, or adapted from television masts; safety is the prime consideration. A very sophisticated 30-metre tower is featured in Cuppers' classic *Hawks in Focus* (Jaclin Enterprises, 1981).

Introducing the hide When using a hide, the observer must be prepared to spend some time in accustoming the birds to the intrusion into their territory. There is no doubt that the time spent will be repaid in full, for a bird that has accepted the hide will behave normally, without fear, provided it is not aware of the observer inside.

It is necessary to introduce the hide gradually, so that it is accepted completely before observation or photography begins. It is most worthwhile to put up a bag 30–50 metres away from a nest or waterhole, ensuring that it is secured so that it doesn't flap, and that it is visible from the focal point. At a nest, always watch from a distance to ensure that the male and female visit without reluctance. At the distance mentioned, we have found only two species that have reacted

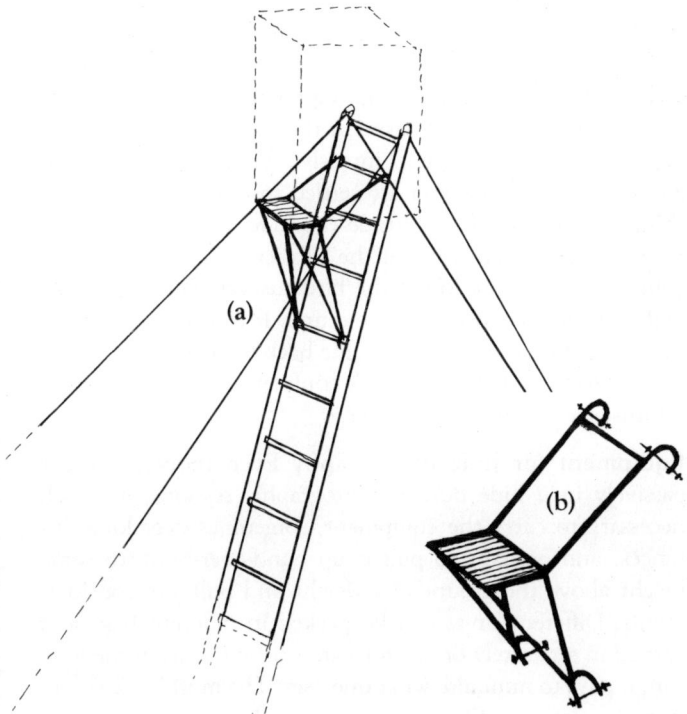

Fig. 18
*(a) Self-standing ladder; (b) seat for top of extended ladder —
lean ladder slightly forward so body is over centre of gravity
when seated.*

at all — the White-backed Swallow and the Swamp Harrier. (I would not recommend any intrusion by observers or photographers into the territory of the latter bird. In the case of the swallow, a dummy hide placed a hundred metres or so away prior to egg laying, and not moved up at all until the chicks are well grown, is the recommended procedure. Without high-speed flash there is little point in photographing the swallow anyway, because it does not pause at the entrance to the burrow.)

After a day or two, the hide can be moved closer in stages, each time checking that male and female accept the intrusion. Finally, when the hide is in position, the birds should be ignoring it completely. (It is also important to follow the same procedure with dummy flash heads and dummy lens barrels, making sure that the birds accept them thoroughly before you begin photography.)

This may appear to be time consuming, but usually only a few minutes are required each day.

When the time comes for photographic sessions, it is advisable to have a helper to assist in the arrangement of equipment, to tie back (not cut) intrusive foliage and, finally, to go away noisily once you are settled to dupe the birds into thinking you have gone. Inside the hide, it is imperative to sit absolutely quietly even if the subject appears tame — all your advantages are lost if the bird suspects you are inside, and its behaviour becomes unnatural. It is just as important to arrange for your helper to come back to get you out of the hide — nothing destroys a bird's confidence more than seeing an unsuspected human emerging.

Equipment for hide photography Even though one sits passively in a hide during photographic sessions, it is still necessary to carry the equipment, sometimes over long distances, and perhaps to pull it up hand-over-hand to some height above the ground. So weight and bulk are considerations. Different units can be packed in different bags and carried in separately or given to an assistant, but, in the long run, it pays to minimise what one uses. The most basic equipment is a lens, an SLR camera, a tripod and stool to sit on. Once birds accept a hide, it can be located at any convenient distance, so a lens having a focal length of 200–300 mm should cover most situations.

The closest one would need to be with such equipment would be about 1.5 metres for really small birds. Few fixed focal length lenses focus that close, so an extension tube could be useful. Many models of zoom lens focus quite close, so they do not need extra tubes. A good size for a hide zoom would be 100–300 mm. Fixed focal length lenses tend to be sharper and have a wider aperture, but are less versatile than zooms.

Unfortunately, it does not take long to realise that this basic kit has limitations, mostly with respect to lighting. It is very rare to find a nest, a waterhole, or a food source that is perfectly lit by available light, so the next piece of equipment that needs to be considered is a source of artificial light. Most versatile is an electronic flash — used intelligently and sensitively, it is the most valuable tool at the disposal of the nature photographer, but unfortunately it is also the most abused.

Electronic flash The aim in using electronic flash should be to produce a picture in which it is difficult to detect that the flash has been used. Ideally, the only clue should be in the multiple highlights in the eye, and, if possible, that too should be eliminated by judicious placement of flash heads. There are two major faults that indicate unintelligent use of flash — unnecessary flat black backgrounds and unnatural black shadows.

The remedy is simple:
1. The light from the flashes should be balanced with the available light.
2. If the available light is not strong enough (as in rainforest), then flashes are directed on to the background as well as on to the subject.

As long as some semblance of nature is apparent, backgrounds can be dark, particularly effectively if the subject is backlit. The ultimate test is boredom — there is no scope for variety in a black background, but in lit backgrounds there are infinite possibilities of colour, depth of tone, richness, harmony, contrast and lighting effects. One can enjoy a hundred well-lit pictures, but start yawning after four or five 'black' ones.

Lighting techniques Intelligent use of artificial light revolves around placement of flash heads. The least convenient place to mount a flash head is where the equipment manufacturers, by dint of their mounting brackets, want you to put it, namely on top of or alongside the camera. The resulting lighting is flat and two-dimensional. This can be improved in a number of ways. The following methods are of increasing complexity, beginning with the simplest.

1. Fill-in technique: a single flash head is used to add light to the shadows thrown by the available light. Film perceives less detail in shadows than the human eye, so a fill-in flash brings the scene closer to human perceptions by lighting up details the camera would otherwise miss. There are degrees of fill-in, depending on the sort of effect it is desired to create, ranging from weak to strong fill-in that is controlled by the distance of the flash from the subject. The harmony of the picture is often increased if a handkerchief or piece of tissue is placed over the flash, softening its light. Quite nice effects can be achieved if a warm filter is also placed over the flash, for example, pale orange or brown (but it can be overdone and cool colours such as blue or purple invariably look wrong). The logical place to set up the fill-in flash is on the opposite side of the camera to the direction of the sun. For the first film or two, vary the strength and angle of the fill-in flash, making a note of what is being done. Studying the results will indicate the combination that is most pleasing. As a starting point, the camera is exposed for the available light, with the flash head placed to give one less f-stop. For example, if the available light reading on the subject is 1/125 at f11, place the flash so it gives f8.

   Set the camera on 1/125 at f11 and take a series of shots as a test. The flash can be placed at different distances and angles to produce light ranging from f11 down to about f4 or f5.6. Probably the best results will be those where there is *not* a complete balance between available light and flash, nor those where the shadows dominate, but somewhere in between.

2. Synchro-sun technique: an extension of the fill-in technique but using more than one flash head. Its optimum use is if the subject is in the shade but the background is sunlit. The flashes are used to match the light on the subject to that on the background.

   If a back-light is not used, all that is required is to take an exposure reading on the background, then position the flashes so that they provide a similar amount of light for the subject. One flash head is not enough, because it will throw a black shadow and, as previously noted this is one of the worst sins in bird photography. So regard one flash as if it were the sun, placing it to one side and higher than the camera, and regard the other as a fill-in flash, to throw light into the shadows cast by the first. So place the 'fill-in' flash on the other side of the camera and also higher.

If a back-light is used, drama can be added to the picture by adding a third light, this time behind and above the subject so it is highlighted. To be used most successfully, the background needs to be darker than the subject, so the flashes are placed to add about one f-stop more to the subject. For example, if the background reading is 1/125 at f8, arrange the front lights so they give f11 and the back light to give f11–16 or f16. Take the pictures at 1/125 at f11.

3. Total lighting: where the subject and the background are heavily shaded, the subject *and* the background need to be flash-lit. If only the subject is lit, the background will be black (tut-tut). So the lighting on the subject will be set up for the synchro-sun technique, but an additional flash or flashes will be used for the background. This can be done in either of two ways, both involving the identification through the ground glass of the patch of background that needs to be lit.

Place one or more flashes near the appropriate background, pointing at it, and attach the synchro cord to a photo-cell release, which is pointed back at the main flash. Photo-cell releases are available from camera stores and are not expensive.

Use a fresnel screen with a flash and direct it at the background area (see p. 59 for details of fresnel screen). The size of the lit area can be adjusted by moving the fresnel screen in relation to the flash. If the background area is large, several flashes may be needed to fill it, but generally one or two will provide enough highlights to suggest a natural background. We have lit backgrounds up to 15–20 metres behind the subjects, using these methods. Don't forget to test that all the flashes are working by manually firing the main head.

Another solution, if background lighting is not possible, is to use an artificial background, but only as a last resort. Some of the most horrendous bird pictures ever taken involve artificial backgrounds, so some taste is required in their employment. Once or twice we have used a sheet of hardboard painted brown and splashed sparsely with orange, ochre, gold and blue paint, giving a pleasant effect of sunlit forest. Avoid at all costs a plain artificial background, particularly blue, since they just don't look right. The secret is to have a natural-looking background, positioned well behind the subject so it is completely out of focus, and light it with its own flash.

Guide numbers To determine what distance the flashes need to be from the subject for correct exposure, it is necessary to work out a guide number, which is the distance of the flash multiplied by the f-stop.

Each flash unit has a manufacturers' guide number, which is based on use in a room providing bounceback of light from the walls. This guide number is not necessarily relevant for use outdoors, so tests need to be carried out to determine a guide number suited to your requirements. Set up the flashes at 1.5 metres from some appropriate subject, such as a group of flowers. Using your preferred film in the camera, take a series of shots starting at the largest aperture on the lens, moving down a half stop for each successive shot until reaching the smallest aperture (f32 or f22). While doing this test, I like to place in the picture area a piece of paper indicating the f-stop being used, changing the paper for each shot. Then repeat the test with the flashes placed at 2 metres. When having the film developed, ask for it to be returned in a strip (for Kodachrome, cut off the corner of the mailer in the place indicated). Now check which frames are correctly exposed. Note the f-stop indicated in the best exposure for the first test and multiply by 1.5: this will give the guide number (distance 1.5 metres × f-stop). Then do the same with the 2 metre test, but multiply the f-stop by 2 to get the guide number (distance 2 metres × f-stop). The guide number from the two tests should be the same.

To work out how far to place the flashes from the subject for any given f-stop, divide the f-stop into the guide number (GN); the result gives the distance. For example, with a guide number of 22, the distance needed for f11 is 2 metres (GN 22 divided by f-stop 11 = 2).

To work out the f-stop, if the flash is at a given distance, divide the guide number by the distance; the result gives the f-stop, for example, with a guide number of 16, the f-stop needed if the flashes are at 1.5 metres is f10.7, or near enough to f11 (GN 16 divided by distance 1.5 = 10.7). Most flashes nowadays have an automatic function which makes the placement of flashes much easier in many instances; however, the subject does not always throw back enough light to cause the correct automatic exposure; an example would be a robin's nest. So it is preferable to work from guide numbers — it doesn't take long to work out a good technique.

The basic kit is building up, now including at least one flash and possibly as many as five with assorted cords and photo-cell releases. If a number of flash heads are to be used, it may pay to purchase a unit that has multiple heads, solving the problem of how to fire them. If individual units are to be used, they can be fired by coupling them, via long synchro cords, to a three-way synchro plug attached to the camera, or via photo-cell releases. Synchro cords are the weakest point of any flash system, so have plenty of spares if they are used, discarding any that malfunction.

Photo-cells will not always operate in sunlight but can be mounted in black film canisters to provide protection from direct sunlight. Infra-red models are more efficient but more expensive and require an infra-red flash to fire them, adding extra bulk.

'TWITCHING'

The world's leading birdwatcher, William Oddie, defines a 'twitcher' as 'one . . . who is openly concerned with adding more and more species to his [or her] list'. Twitchers regard a new bird added to the list as a 'tick'. If it is a new bird for Australia, it is a 'mega-tick'. Subspecies are regarded as 'mini-ticks'. A tick looks like this ✓; this is a mega-tick ✔ and this is a mini-tick ✓.

Twitchers, in common with cricketers, thrive on milestones, usually associated with fifties or hundreds. The elite birdwatchers in Australia are those who have exceeded 600 Australian species; those who achieve this distinction are eligible for election to the '600 Club'. Only the utmost dedication makes possible the next major milestone, 700; consequently, there are only one or two '700 Clubbers' so far.

Apart from adding birds to the list, twitchers also enjoy other activities, such as listing the number of species observed in a day, a month or a year. Roy Wheeler, when approaching his eightieth birthday, managed 600 Australian species in a calendar year, a prodigious feat.

Occasions of great fun are 'twitch-a-thons', organised by birdwatching clubs for small groups who compete for the greatest number of species seen in a set period, usually 12 hours, 24 hours or 'dawn to dusk'. To dismiss such outings as trivial is to miss the whole point, that is, the honing of observational skills. A similar event, organised on a wider level, is the Challenge Bird Count, when teams enumerate the species seen within a given radius of a city or town over a 24-hour period. To join one of the teams is guaranteed to extend greatly the enjoyment of birdwatching.

EXTENDED OBSERVATIONS

At a more serious level, much enjoyment can be obtained from watching particular birds over a period and noting down the results of the observations. Memory is such a fickle servant that notes should be taken on the spot, not written up later. The main purpose of the notebook is to provide a convenient repository for your observations. There is so much to learn about Australian birds that any observer can add new knowledge. Some potentially productive avenues of observation are mentioned in the following paragraphs; somewhere among the items should be at least one that strikes a sympathetic chord. At first it may seem difficult to decide which observations are relevant, but growing interest will probably send you to the 'literature', which is the term for what other people have written about the subject, either in books or in journals (a list of some of these is given on page 84). Having read what others have observed will give you a clearer idea of how to proceed, as well as providing a terminology. An ideal book to read as a starting point is Ian Rowley's *Bird Life* (Collins, 1974), which discusses discoveries that have been made about some common Australian birds.

Abundance

By choosing a route in some convenient bushland that can be visited regularly, it is possible to build up over a period of

Satin Bowerbird displaying. The iridescent plumage of the male is seen at its best during courtship displays. Although the male prefers to decorate his bower with blue objects, during display when the female is present, he holds yellow leaves or cicada-nymph cases in his bill.

Raoul Slater

Eastern Yellow Robin at nest.

time a fairly clear idea of what species occur there and how many individuals of each species can be expected at different times of the year. The route does not need to be long, but it should be visited at the same time of the day to obtain some relativity.

A typical notebook entry might look like Figure 19.

Relative abundance can be determined in two ways: firstly by adding all the individuals for a given date, then working out the percentage that each species represents of the total. For example, if there are three Yellow Robins in a total of 60 birds counted, then its relative abundance for that date is 5 per cent or, alternatively, by working out the percentage of the total number of trips on which a species was noted.

Density per hectare can be determined by dividing the number of birds by the area covered.

A particularly relevant area of abundance studies is the effect of fire on local populations of birds. A route through a patch of bush that is burnt at intervals could provide valuable information helpful in assessing optimum times for controlled burning.

Arrival and departure dates of migrants

This is probably the simplest form of observation, only requiring that eyes and ears are kept tuned during the appropriate months, August–October and March–April. It is much easier to date arrivals than departures. If kept over many

RELATIVE ABUNDANCE

PLACE	MOGGILL STATE FOREST					
	DATE					
SPECIES	12 JAN	13 FEB	14 MAR	10 MAY	21 JUNE	15 JUL
YELLOW ROBIN	3	3	2	4	3	1
SCARLET ROBIN	1	1	—	—	—	7

Fig. 19

Typical notebook entries on relative abundance.

years, this data may, in conjunction with other people's observations, help to pinpoint migratory routes. Particular features to watch out for are whether male birds arrive before females and whether juveniles leave at the same time as adults. It would also be interesting to know whether individuals of migratory species that fail to leave are juvenile or adults. A typical notebook entry might look like Figure 20.

Distribution

One of the finest co-operative efforts ever undertaken by birdwatchers anywhere resulted in the *Atlas of Australian Birds* by Blakers, Davies and Reilly (Melbourne University Press, 1984), incorporating the observations of more than 3000 observers over a five-year period, pinpointing the known distributional limits of all Australian birds. The *Atlas* not only shows where birds have been recorded, but also indicates areas where further observations may extend the boundaries of known distributions. If visiting a new area, perusal of the *Atlas* will show which species to expect and also any species that are recorded nearby but not at that particular spot.

Roosting

Very few observations have been recorded concerning roosting behaviour. Admittedly, it is a difficult area of study, but watching in the late evening (accompanied by a torch) could reveal where birds sleep and any behaviour associated with

MIGRANT ARRIVALS AND DEPARTURES

PLACE MOGGILL STATE FOREST						
SPECIES	Year 1986		Year 1987		Year 1988	
	Arr.	Dep.	Arr.	Dep.	Arr.	Dep.
ROSE ROBIN	15·4	22·8	12·4	25·8	14·4	16·8
CHANNEL- BILLED CUCKOO	30·9	—	14·10	16·4	28·9	12·4

Fig. 20
Typical notebook entries on migrant birds.

roosting. Frogmouths, which roost during the day, could provide an interesting study. Some are not infrequently found roosting on the ground; one Papuan Frogmouth, for example, was found to use approximately the same spot over a period of five days. Is such behaviour normal? The large coastal Tawny Frogmouth appears not to roost on the ground at all, but the small inland Tawny does occasionally. Why the difference?

Feeding

Feeding is an enormous subject and its study could fill many lifetimes. For the average birdwatcher it revolves around three possible questions:

1. What are the feeding methods?
2. What is consumed?
3. How much constitutes a daily ration?

Of these three, it is easiest to build up knowledge about the ways in which birds feed, requiring only observation and some descriptive ability. Identification of the food eaten is simpler for plant, fruit and seed eaters, for samples can be taken. The problem is much greater with invertebrate food. Perhaps the way the amateur can best assist is in photographing birds feeding their chicks. By concentrating the focus of the photograph on the food and by noting how often each chick is fed, some useful information can be obtained.

Such information is biased, however, towards whatever food is most readily available at the time and may have little relevance to what might be consumed at other times of the year. For example, a pair of Red-backed Wrens we watched for several days fed their chicks entirely on one species of spider but obviously the birds' territory would not support such specific predation for long.

To determine how much is eaten requires watching individual birds for a whole day at a time, probably most productively with species eating food items of a known weight, such as seeds, native figs and grasshoppers.

Drinking and bathing

Watching at a waterhole over extended periods not only provides close-up views of birds but can add information about an often neglected aspect of a bird's daily routine. Choice of waterholes is obviously important; best observations are obtained if it is the only source of water in the area, resulting in a fairly accurate idea of how many birds occur nearby. By colour-banding individuals, it is possible to determine how far they travel to water and how often they drink.

Observation should not involve disturbance, so is best carried out from a hide. As there are occasions on which many birds arrive together, making note-taking difficult, it is perhaps easiest to keep a tally by speaking into a tape recorder, noting the time at frequent intervals, then transferring the information on to a table or into a computer later.

One surprising feature is which species in an area do *not* visit the waterhole. Cuckoo-shrikes, trillers, cuckoos, sittellas and Little Shrike-thrush are some locally abundant birds that were not observed at a particular waterhole watched regularly over a ten-year period.

Fig. 21
Budgerigar at waterhole.

Predation

Generally one does not set out to study predation on birds, because such occurrences are not frequently observed, but notes should be kept on any instances that do occur. Victims of birds of prey are often difficult to identify unless the attack is witnessed, because they are quickly plucked. It is possible to identify some small birds from skulls in owl and raptor pellets. A productive source of information is a sparrow-hawk's plucking perch. Unsuccessful attacks by raptores do not necessarily reflect the dietary preferences of the attacker, because birds of prey often chase other birds in play, including species they have never been known to kill. Predation by other animals on birds is not often recorded; apart from the domestic and feral cat, goannas, snakes (particularly Brown Tree-snake), lizards, tortoises, fish, crocodiles, rats and possums have been mentioned. Many bird nests, particularly in rainforest, are subject to predation, but few observations have been made concerning the culprits. As many nests are raided at night, some form of mechanical device, such as a photo-cell attached to a camera, would be needed to find out what causes the damage.

A regular 'predator' on some species of birds is the motor car. Notes kept on road kills can indicate vulnerable species and times of the year when they are most at risk, but will probably not decrease the number killed each year.

Daily routine

By following an individual bird for long periods, an idea may be formed of its daily routine — how much time is spent feeding, preening, resting, drinking, bathing, interacting, singing and flying. A suitable species to study would be one that is fairly localised in open habitat, where it can be kept in view for the period of study and where it is not likely to be confused with another bird. Ideally, the bird should be marked in some way to make it identifiable, for example, by colour-banding or with a tag. However, permission to band or mark a bird is not necessarily easy to obtain and there are penalties for marking a bird without permission, so it is possibly best to study unmarked birds for a while to find out if this field of study appeals to you. Some serious intent would need to be shown before a banding permit would be issued and the co-operation of a registered bander would be required to affix the appropriate rings.

Breeding

Breeding is regarded by many as the most productive field for study — both short-term and long-term projects. The scope of involvement can range from the entire field of breeding behaviour to the study of one particular aspect.

Courtship display Birds tend to be possessive of the space about them and many have developed displays to warn others against encroaching into it, thus avoiding the necessity for outright aggression; the encroaching bird may adopt an 'appeasement' display to indicate it does not want a dispute. The function of courtship displays is to permit the pair of birds to encroach into each other's personal space without triggering aggression. Displays are often derived from other activities, such as feeding, drinking, wiping the beak or preening, becoming ritualised in the process. Ducks are good subjects to start an interest in displays, as there is a helpful book *The Handbook of Waterfowl Behaviour* by P. A. Johnsgard (Constable, 1965), in which different displays are illustrated, described and named. One of the problems in studying displays is in finding out if that particular display has been recorded before, whether it has been described in detail and whether a name has been coined for it. A good source of information is *The Handbook of the Birds of Europe and the Middle East and North Africa*, edited by Stanley Cramp (Oxford University Press). It is a work of several volumes, as yet incomplete. While it discusses Western Palaearctic birds, its summaries of the behaviour of the individual species include names of displays that can be adopted for similar Australian birds. It is a very expensive book and is perhaps, initially, best consulted in a library.

Birds that perform spectacular displays are herons and egrets, frigatebirds, cormorants, pelicans, terns, birds of prey, bowerbirds, lyrebirds and riflebirds. Bowerbirds, in particular, are fine subjects for study as at least one species occurs in most parts of northern and eastern Australia and the period during which displays occur extends over much of the year in some species.

Courtship feeding One element of pair-bonding is feeding of the female by the male. The female often postures in a manner similar to a chick begging for food, which may have a function in appeasing aggression. A more prosaic function is to allow the female to build up body reserves preparatory to egg laying and to anticipate the incubation period when the female is fed on the nest to save her leaving the eggs unattended. It would be interesting to compare the nesting routine of similar species, one of which indulges in courtship feeding and the other does not, for example, Spotted Catbird and Satin Bowerbird. In birds of prey, courtship feeding is important, and may precede egg laying for many months. Female raptores are often much bigger and more powerful than males; a Grey Goshawk female has been observed eating a male. Observations on Collared Sparrowhawks suggest that, early in the season (April–May), the male will not attempt to mate with the female unless she is holding some food he has given her.

Nest-site selection Picking an appropriate site for a nest is obviously of great relevance to successful breeding, but there are not many records of the way Australian birds go about it. Note such factors as length of time taken, number of potential sites examined and whether selection is determined by male or female.

Nest building Features to watch for are whether both sexes build, how the material is gathered, how often it is brought, how long the incorporation of each item takes, how long it takes to complete the nest, the way it is constructed, an estimation or actual count of the number of pieces included and what they consist of. I recall helping Dr Klaus Immelmann to itemise the material used in a Red-eared Firetail's nest and we found one piece of grass almost a metre long; it consisted of a main stem with over a hundred sub-stems, leaflets and tendrils. How the bird manoeuvred it into position in the nest site 15 metres above the ground remains in my mind as a tribute to its persistence; the fact that the nest contained nearly 2000 pieces indicated the enormous expenditure of energy required for its construction. Study of nest building should be tempered by the fact that some species will abandon their efforts if disturbed — watching from a distance with a telescope obviates this risk. Some particularly vulnerable species are pigeons, fantails and flycatchers.

Egg laying and incubation This phase of study is also prone to tragic conclusions — some birds should not be disturbed at all while incubating. These include all endangered species (lists available from most State National Parks and Wildlife Services, or in *Rare and Vanishing Australian Birds* by Peter Slater, Rigby, 1978), all native pigeons and doves, fantails, Swamp Harrier and Peregrine Falcon. Even with species that do not readily desert their eggs, it is somewhat doubtful if some of the information gathered, for example, the interval between eggs being laid and the incubation period, is worth the risk, due to the fact that the disturbance caused by checking may disrupt the normal pattern enough to modify the results. Some information *can* be obtained without disturbance, for example, whether both male and female incubate and for what period; how long the nest is left unattended under natural circumstances; how often the eggs are turned; how does the incubating bird deal with ants; is material added to the nest during the incubation period and does any reshaping occur?

The Royal Australasian Ornithologists' Union conducts a nest record scheme and provides cards for the compilation of data.

Fledging Once the eggs hatch, the quiescence of the incubation period gives way to the frenetic activities of the fledging period, when the chicks have to be alternately brooded and fed. There are two sorts of fledgling — those that leave the nest shortly after hatching (precocial), usually covered

NEST RECORD CHART

SPECIES	Building		Eggs Laid					Hatch	Fledge
	Start	Finish	1	2	3	4	5		
YELLOW ROBIN	6-8-87 MOGGILL STATE FOREST								
	6-8	15-8	17-8	18-8				2-9	17-9
BROWN THORNBILL	8-8-87 MOGGILL STATE FOREST								
	—	—	12-8	13-8	14-8			27-8	9-9
VARIEGATED WREN	12-8-87 MOGGILL STATE FOREST								
	—	14-8	17-8	18-8	19-8			1-9	14-9
WILLIE WAGTAIL	15-8-87 KANGAROO GULLY RD								
	—	20-8	23/8	24/8	26/8			8-9/9-9	24-9

Fig. 22

Typical notebook entries in nest record chart.

with patterned down, born with eyes open and able to feed themselves within a few days, and those that remain in the nest (altricial), usually naked or sparsely covered with down, usually born with unopened eyes and requiring to be fed by the parents for at least three weeks. Observations are much easier with altricial young as they remain localised in the nest, but care must be taken not to disrupt the normal pattern. Therefore, the use of a hide is of particular importance. To determine what is being fed to the chicks requires the hide to be close, but to watch other activities, such as length of brooding periods, changeover, removal of droppings, timing and frequency of feeding, the hide can be further away. In finding out the length of the fledging period, it is imperative not to disturb the nest when the chicks are big, as they may leave prematurely, which not only subtracts from their chances of survival but skews the result. A typical notebook entry is shown in Figure 22.

Most altricial fledglings continue to be fed by the parents after they have left the nest, but it is usually difficult to record precisely for how long. A final item of interest is how long the young birds remain with their parents once they become self-sufficient.

Co-operative breeding
One particular aspect of breeding that merits further study is the large number of Australian birds that have 'helpers' at the nest, in most cases immature birds from previous nests. Birds that breed co-operatively include kookaburras, kingfishers, megapodes, bee-eaters, swallows, sittellas, treecreepers, babblers, cuckoo-shrikes, flycatchers, wrens, warblers, honeyeaters, flower-peckers, pardalotes, mud-nest builders, woodswallows, magpies and butcherbirds. Not all species within these groups breed in co-operation; the list of those that do is probably not complete.

Plumage development
Many birds go through plumage stages before reaching adulthood and some wear different plumages at different times of the year (see pp. 37–40). Two particularly fascinating species in Australia are polymorphic, that is, they have a number of adult plumage forms. They are the Brown Falcon and the Tawny Frogmouth. Notes kept on which forms occur where may help to establish a pattern of occurrence.

Moult
This is an extension of the previous study, involving the timing of the changes from one plumage to another. It is very much a study associated with bird-banding, for the best way of determining the stage of moult is with a bird in the hand. It is of great value in banding because it can help to pinpoint the precise age of the bird that has been caught for ringing. Thus a Wedgetailed Eagle in second-year plumage with primaries one, two and three (counting from inside out) fresh and four missing could be about 17½ months old.

Sounds
Basically, the sounds uttered by birds can be divided into four categories:
1. calls, which are used to communicate meaning other than breeding;
2. songs, which are used for activities associated with breeding;
3. subsongs or 'whisper songs', which basically seem to communicate well-being;
4. mechanical sounds such as feather rattling, bill-clapping, usually used in displays, for courtship or aggression.

   The study of bird sounds can be pursued with equal enjoyment at any level from the most superficial to the most complex, from artistic to scientific, and can involve anything from odd weekend sallies with a cheap tape recorder to fulltime employment with a laboratory full of equipment.

Territory
Territories are maintained by birds for breeding and/or for feeding. Proclamation and defence of territory is usually done by means of song, but displays and combat may also occur. Studies of territory involve determining the size of the territory, the period of the year for which it is maintained, whether male and female are involved in territorial defence, whether 'helpers' in co-operative species also help defend the territory and what other species are attacked.

   There are various categories of territory:
1. combined feeding, mating and nesting, for example, Eastern Yellow Robin;
2. mating and nesting, where feeding is away from the nesting area, for example, Crimson Chat;
3. mating, for example, Spotted Bowerbird;

4. feeding, for example, Darter;
5. roosting, for example, lorikeets.

Life history

The ultimate form of bird study is to attempt to detail the entire spectrum of the life of a species. Most of the Australian birds that have been studied in such detail have been those of economic importance, such as shearwaters (muttonbirds), gulls, ducks, quail, crows, eagles, cockatoos, parrots, finches, cormorants, darter and ibis, or as part of the academic process in universities, for example, terns, herons, miners, kookaburras, some honeyeaters and birds of prey. But there is unlimited scope for interested amateurs. Choice of a subject would most profitably be one that has not been studied in detail before. *The Mallee Fowl* by H. J. Frith (Angus & Robertson, 1962) and *Kookaburras* by Veronica Parry (Lansdowne, 1970) are very readable accounts of such studies, a number of which are also summarised in *Bird Life* by Ian Rowley (Collins, 1974).

Before contemplating working on a life history, an amateur would be well advised to take professional advice. Not everyone is suited to this sort of activity and, I suspect, some sort of tertiary education or its equivalent would be a prerequisite.

Singing Starling

A suitable equivalent would be a thorough knowledge of the literature on bird behaviour. This is not to suggest that bird study is the province of professional ornithologists, but rather to ensure that time is not wasted in fruitless pursuits.

That amateurs can contribute worthily may be gauged by reading such accounts as the following:

Angus Robinson, 'Magpie-larks — A Study in Behaviour', *Emu*, Vol. 46, pp. 265–81; *Emu*, Vol. 47, pp. 11–28, pp. 147–53.

Angus Robinson, 'The Annual Reproductory Cycle of the Magpie ... in South-West Australia', *Emu*, Vol. 56, pp. 233–336.

W. R. Wheeler and I. Watson, 'The Silver Gull *Larus novaehollandiae* Stephens', *Emu*, Vol. 63, pp. 99–173.

R. E. Vallenga, 'Behaviour of the Male Satin Bowerbird at the Bower', *Australian Bird Bander*, Vol. 8, pp. 3–11.

R. E. Vallenga, 'Moults of the Satin Bowerbird *Ptilorhynchus violaceus*', *Emu*, Vol. 80, pp. 49–54.

R. E. Vallenga, 'Distribution of the Satin Bowerbird at Leura, NSW', *Emu*, Vol. 80, pp. 97–102.

Jack and Lindsay Cupper, *Hawks in Focus*, Jaclin Enterprises, Mildura, 1981.

Pauline Reilly, *Fairy Penguins and Earthy People*, Lothian, 1983.

David Hollands, *Eagles, Hawks and Falcons of Australia*, Nelson, 1984.

These are only a few of many works, but they are sufficient to serve as an inspiration to us all.

SUSPECTED NEW BIRD

Every birdwatcher, I am sure, dreams of adding a new bird to the Australian list, whether it is a migrant/vagrant from elsewhere, or a totally new species. However, few observers are sure of the steps that should be taken to verify the sighting and to publish the record. Below are a few thoughts.

Take a detailed description This will include everything that you can note about the bird and the circumstances of its discovery:

1. Date, time, place, weather conditions, distance, make and size of binoculars or telescope and companions should be noted.

2. Note the size of the bird, shape, colour and length of bill and legs. Note the colour and patterns on head, nape, back, rump, upper-tail coverts, upper tail; throat, breast, belly, vent, undertail coverts, undertail; scapulars, lesser wing coverts, greater wing coverts, secondaries, primaries; in flight, any prominent markings such as pale bars or 'windows' in wings.
3. Make a sketch, however roughly, showing where patterns and markings occur.
4. If with companions, ask them to make independent notes without referring to yours. A new record is more likely to be accepted if more than one observer saw it.

Check possibilities There are several possibilities:
1. It is a colour phase or plumage of an Australian bird that is unknown to you.
2. It is an aberrant example of an Australian bird, such as:
   (a) an albino or lutino, or partial albino/lutino (an albino loses structural colours such as blues and violets, as well as pigments forming browns and blacks but may retain some of the pigment colours such as red and orange; while a lutino is an albino that has retained yellow pigment — usually it is derived from a green bird);
   (b) a green bird that has lost yellow pigment, in which case the green parts of the normal plumage will be blue and the yellow parts will be white;
   (c) a dark-plumaged bird that has lost eumelanin (black) pigment and appears brown where the normal bird is black or dark grey.
3. It is discoloured. Sometimes, birds become stained with unusual colours, for example, cormorants and ducks that swim in water rich in iron or tannin become rust-coloured; gulls may be marked with oil; honeyeaters often have a yellow or orange dusting of pollen usually concentrated on the forehead and nape; woodswallows and trillers are often seen with foreheads yellow or orange from contact with pollen.
4. It is an escaped aviary bird. Many foreign species of finches, pigeons, doves and parrots are kept in captivity and could escape. If the strange bird belongs to one of these groups, check a book on cagebirds such as *Cage and*

Aviary Birds by R. M. Martin (Collins, 1984).

5. It is a migratory bird blown off course. The most likely examples are seabirds, waders and ducks, but a number of small perching birds are also possibilities, species that regularly migrate from Asia to Indonesia, for example, Eastern Crowned Warbler, Brown Shrike, Siberian Rubythroat. If the bird is a seabird (petrel, shearwater, albatross, gull or tern), check Peter Harrison's *Seabirds* (Croom Helm, 1983); if a wader, check *Shorebirds* by Hayman, Marchant and Prater (Croom Helm, 1986); if a duck, heron or a small bird, check *A Field Guide to the Birds of South-East Asia* by King, Woodcock & Dickinson (Collins, 1975). It is worth consulting an interesting paper 'Audubon's Shearwater in Australia' by Mike Carter in *Australian Bird Watcher*, Vol. 12 (5), 1988, which details the process of elimination entailed in identifying a difficult species.

6. It is a new species. Several new species have been uncovered in the relatively recent past — Hall's Babbler, Grey Grasswren, Eungella Honeyeater, Mangrove Fantail, Chirruping Wedgebill, Russet-tailed Thrush, Lesser Sooty Owl and the problematical Rusty-tailed Warbler. Most of these are similar to well-known species and were regarded as subspecies of them until further research suggested the possibility that they were new species. The Grey Grasswren was the last previously unsuspected species to be discovered — but there is a distinct possibility that there are more — and grasswrens are the most likely species, being secretive and often localised.

Submitting the record If, after checking all available books, it still appears that it is a 'new' bird for Australia and not an unusually coloured native bird or escapee, there are two possible courses of action.

1. If you have not been able to identify the bird, send copies of all relevant notes, sketches and photographs to the Royal Australasian Ornithologists' Union, for checking by the Record Appraisal Committee. Hopefully they will be able to identify the bird and offer advice as to the next step.

2. If you have been able to identify the bird, write up the details in suitable form and submit it to a recognised bird journal. The editor will then send the 'paper' to the

Record Appraisal Committee and other referees, who will recommend whether or not the record should be published. Probably the best journals are the organs of your State ornithological society, or the *Australian Bird Watcher*. Read back numbers to see how the record should be written up. An excellent example is 'An Australian Record of the Lesser Yellowlegs' by Fred T. H. Smith in the *Australian Bird Watcher*, 10 (4), December 1983. Usually there is some delay in publication, so if you are concerned that someone else may claim the record, you may feel tempted to send prior notice to a newsletter such as the *Bird Observer* for inclusion in their monthly column *Unusual Sightings* — but take the advice in this matter of the editor of the journal in which you wish to publish. There are conventions which can easily be breached by those unused to academic procedure — the editor is concerned for the integrity of his journal, so it is imperative that his advice is heeded to the letter. He will also advise you as to the authorship of the paper, whose names should go on it and in what order (in a case where several people are involved in the discovery).

If the bird you have found is new to science, the procedure is different and contains an unpalatable aspect, namely the taking of specimens. A description of a new species has to be based on a specimen, ideally backed up by one or more additional specimens to indicate that it is not a 'sport' and to show variety of plumage. This is best left to the State museum ornithologist, who, having verified your discovery, will obtain the necessary permits, collect, prepare and house the specimens. The specimen on which the description is based will be called the 'type' and the others taken at the same time will be 'co-types'. It is preferable if the ornithologist at the museum becomes involved in the preparation of the 'paper', as he will be aware of the proper procedure and will be able to suggest a suitable name for the bird. In this case, the paper will be submitted to an appropriate journal in the names of the discoverer and the ornithologist, and these names will follow that of the bird, for example, Grey Grasswren *Amytornis barbatus* Favaloro and McEvey, 1968. (Once again, there are conventions of procedure which the ornithologist will explain to you and which must not be breached.) Alternatively, the ornithologist may suggest that the bird is named after you, in which case you cannot be involved in the paper describing the bird, for example, Rufous Bristlebird *Dasyornis broadbenti* (McCoy 1867), named after the discoverer, Kendall Broadbent, by Dr McCoy, founder and first Director of the National Museum, Melbourne. However, I would suggest that, in the unlikely event that you are asked if the bird's vernacular name should be in your honour in preference to the scientific name, for example, Jones's Warbler, that you consider the matter carefully, because a common name can be changed later but a scientific name cannot. In general, I disagree with the notion of birds being named after people. Bird names should have some descriptive meaning, thus it is, in my view, better if you accept the first course of action and are cited as co-author of the paper describing the bird. It is possible to collect the specimen and prepare the paper yourself, but this is not a course that I would recommend to the average birdwatcher.

Some of the black and white illustrations of birds appearing in *The Birdwatcher's Notebook* include species which are not represented in *The Slater Field Guide to Australian Birds*, as they were discovered after the publication of the *Field Guide*.

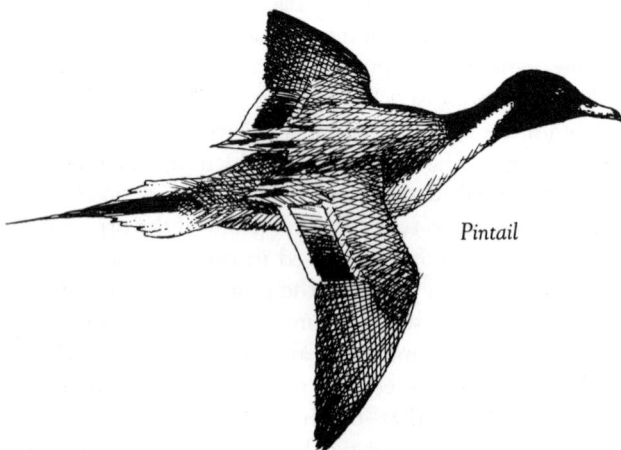

Pintail

LIBRARY

There are so many books about Australian birds that it is difficult to know which should be included in a personal library. It would be nice to have them all, but as a starting point, here are some that summarise current knowledge and could form the basis of a collection. The books are categorised as follows:

*** essential
** essential if interested in subject
* include if funds permit

Basic texts

*** *Reader's Digest Book of Australian Birds*, R. Schodde (ed.), 2nd edn, Reader's Digest, 1986.

*** *Fundamentals of Ornithology*, J. Van Tyne & A. J. Berger, Wiley, 1959.

*** *The Atlas of Australian Birds*, M. Blakers, S. J. J. F. Davies & P. N. Reilly, Melbourne University Press, 1984.

and/or (depending on area of interest):

** *The Tasmanian Bird Atlas*, D. G. Thomas, University of Tasmania, Hobart, 1979.

** *Atlas of Victorian Birds*, W. B. Emison, C. M. Beardsell, F. I. Norman & R. H. Loyn, Ministry of Conservation, Forests and Lands and Royal Australasian Ornithologists' Union, 1987.

*** *Where to Find Birds in Australia*, J. Bransbury, Century Hutchinson, 1988.

* *The Great Australian Birdfinder*, M. Morcombe, Lansdowne, 1986.

** *The Illustrated Dictionary of Australian Birds by Common Names*, J. D. MacDonald, Reed, 1987. (Gives derivations of bird names.)

Field guides

*** *The Slater Field Guide to Australian Birds*, Peter, Pat & Raoul Slater, Rigby, 1986.

used in conjunction with

*** *A Field Guide to the Birds of Australia*, G. Pizzey, Collins, 1980.

*** *What Bird is That?*, N. W. Cayley (revised by Terence R. Lindsey), Angus & Robertson, 1984.
* *The Birds of Australia*, K. Simpson & N. Day, 2nd edn, Viking O'Neil, 1986.
* *Australia, Land of Birds*, D. & M. Trounson, Collins, 1987.

Behaviour
** *Bird Life*, I. Rowley, Collins, 1974.
** *Understanding Australian Birds*, J. D. MacDonald, Reed, 1982.

Species accounts
** *The Mallee Fowl*, H. J. Frith, Angus & Robertson, 1962.
** *Waterfowl in Australia*, H. J. Frith, Angus & Robertson, 1967.
** *Pigeons and Doves of Australia*, H. J. Frith, Rigby, 1982.
** *Kookaburras*, V. Parry, Lansdowne, 1970.
** *Shorebirds*, P. Hayman, J. Marchant & T. Prater, Croom Helm, 1986.
and/or
* *Shorebirds in Australia*, B. Lane, Nelson, 1987.

** *Seabirds, an Identification Guide*, P. Harrison, Croom Helm/Reed, 1983.
** *Hawks in Focus*, J. & L. Cupper, Jaclin Enterprises, Mildura, 1980.
* *Eagles, Hawks and Falcons of Australia*, D. Hollands, Nelson, 1984.
** *Nightwatchmen of Bush and Plain*, D. Fleay, Jacaranda, 1968.
** *Australian Parrots*, J. M. Forshaw & W. T. Cooper, 2nd rev. edn, Lansdowne, 1981.
* *Nocturnal Birds of Australia*, R. Schodde & I. J. Mason, Lansdowne, 1980.
* *The Fairy Wrens*, R. Schodde & R. Weatherley, Lansdowne, 1982.
** *Australian Finches*, K. Immelmann, Angus & Robertson, 1982.

Extra-Australian texts
*** *The Birds of Papua New Guinea Vol. I*, B. J. Coates, Dove Publications, 1985. (Not only authoritative but also aesthetically pleasing.)

* *Birds of New Guinea*, B. M. Beehler, T. K. Pratt & D. Z. Zimmerman, Princeton University Press, 1986. (Many birds are common to New Guinea and Australia.)
* *Reader's Digest Complete Book of New Zealand Birds*, C. J. R. Robertson, Reader's Digest, 1985.

Photographic

* Volumes produced by the National Photographic Index of Australian Wildlife, containing many beautiful photographs and well-written summaries of information:
  Wrens and Warblers of Australia
  The Waterbirds of Australia
  The Seabirds of Australia
  The Shorebirds of Australia
  The Robins and Flycatchers of Australia

* *The Techniques of Bird Photography*, J. Warham, 3rd edn, Focal Press, 1973.
* *Masterpieces of Australian Bird Photography*, Peter Slater, Rigby, 1980.

Classics

There are some classic books of yore (most of them, unfortunately, out of print), that round out the library, including:
  A Natural History of Selborne, Gilbert White.
  Territory in Bird Life, Eliot Howard.
  Bird Display and Behaviour, E. A. Armstrong.
  A Herring Gull's World, Niko Tinbergen.
  Handbook to the Birds of Australia, John Gould.
  Bush Charms, L. G. Chandler.

Common Koel

CHECKLIST OF AUSTRALIAN BIRDS

One of the most pleasant ways of remembering a birdwatching trip is to refer back to a list of the birds observed. On the following pages is a checklist of Australian birds, arranged in the same order as they occur and giving the page reference in *The Slater Field Guide to Australian Birds*. There are a number of squares for ticks, enabling you to keep a permanent record of a substantial number of forays into the wild. (This checklist and the other blank charts may be photocopied for your own personal use before using them to increase the number of birdwatching trips that can be recorded.) It is suggested that the first square be kept as a 'life-list'. After the checklist there is an index for sixty trips where details such as date, place, weather, companions and so on can be recorded.

Birds have always inspired enough interest for people to give them common or vernacular names. These names may be affectionate (Jacky Winter, Willy Wagtail); derisive (booby, noddy); hybrid (cuckoo-shrike); descriptive (swift); alien (Baza); academic (cisticola); ridiculous (Henna-hooded Foliage-gleaner); inspirational (Shining Sunbeam); onomatopoeic (kookaburra); ecological (Spinifexbird) and so on. In different areas of a country, people often have different names for the same bird, making communication about them difficult. Thus it seems good sense to have one 'official' common name for each bird, so that birdwatchers anywhere within a country, or even overseas, can communicate.

The Royal Australasian Ornithologists' Union determines which names are official in Australia. Its first checklist, published in 1911, amended an earlier list produced by the Australian Academy for the Advancement of Science in 1896, before the Union was formed. Neither of these lists met with universal approval and so a new Vernacular Names Committee was formed, resulting in a Checklist of Australian birds in 1926 that standardised common names for more than half a century. However, many of these names were parochial, for example, the bird known in Australia as the Marsh Crake was known in other countries as Baillon's

Crake. So, in a number of publications, attempts were made to bring Australian names into line with international convention. At the same time, certain names, deemed inappropriate, were 'updated'.

On the face of it such moves should have met with immediate approval, but such is the nature of human obstinacy (exemplified by the number of people who still refer to their height in feet and inches and have no idea of how tall they are in centimetres) that it will be years before the 'old' names die out. As much as individuals dislike the 'new' names, their eventual adoption is inevitable, so the sooner one begins to use them the better. In *The Slater Field Guide* we decided on an evolutionary course — in the first edition new names were introduced in brackets after the old. In our second edition (and in this volume, with some exceptions) we reverse the procedure, with the old names in brackets after the new and, hopefully, in the third edition the old names can be dropped altogether.

The exceptions referred to in this volume are where academic names have been advocated for vernacular names, for example, the names Hylacola for heathwrens and Calamanthus for fieldwrens. Both of these names are now out of date in scientific terms and would be better replaced by the simpler and more accurate title of Scrubwren. In this checklist we have placed them in brackets after the 'old' name and leave it up to each observer as to which is used. Apart from these exceptions, academic or scientific names are omitted altogether from this list in the interests of brevity.

To add more interest to birdwatching, we have included a number of sub-species or 'forms' that are readily identifiable in the field. Some of them, with further investigation, will be found to be valid species in their own right. Details of how to identify them are found in *The Slater Field Guide* and other guides.

	Page ref.*	Life-list	64						
Southern Cassowary	10	✓							
Emu	10								
Ostrich	10								
Hoary-headed Grebe	12	✓		✓					
Australasian Grebe (little)	12	✓		✓					
Great crested Grebe	12	✓							
King Penguin	14								
Gentoo Penguin	14								
Adelie Penguin	14								
Chinstrap Penguin	14								
Magellanic Penguin	14								
Little Penguin	14								
Erect-crested Penguin	16								
Rockhopper Penguin	16								
eastern form									
western form									
Fiordland Penguin	16								
Snares Penguin	16								
Royal Penguin	16								
Black-browed Albatross	18								
dark-eyed form									
pale-eyed form									
Grey-headed Albatross	18								
Running Total									

* Page references refer to *The Slater Field Guide to Australian Birds*, Peter, Pat & Raoul Slater, Rigby, 1986.

CHECKLIST OF AUSTRALIAN BIRDS

30 31 Nov 1. 2 3. 4 5 6

					✓								
	✓												
						✓							

95

SYDNEY | AYER'S ROCK | DARW
(ULURU) | KAK

Oct. 23 24 | 25 26 27 28 29

	Page ref.*	Life-list							
Yellow-nosed Albatross	18								
Buller's Albatross	18								
Shy Albatross	18								
Australian form									
grey-backed form									
Chatham Islands form									
Sooty Albatross	20								
Light-mantled Sooty Albatross	20								
Royal Albatross	20								
northern form									
southern form									
Wandering Albatross	20								
Southern Giant Petrel	20								
Northern Giant Petrel	20								
Southern (Antarctic) Fulmar	22								
Antarctic Petrel	22								
Cape Petrel	22								
Snow Petrel	22								
Grey Petrel	22								
White-chinned Petrel	24								
dark-eyed form									
ring-eyed form									
Black Petrel	24								
Running Total									

U | BRISBANE | TOWNSVILLE & MISSION BEACH | TABLELANDS (MALANDA) & CAIRNS
BINNABURRA LODGE

30 31 1 2 3 4 5 6 7 8 9

	Page ref.*	Life-list								
Westland Petrel	24									
Kerguelen Petrel	24									
Providence Petrel	24									
Great-winged Petrel	24									
Australian form										
NZ form										
Tahiti Petrel	26									
Atlantic Petrel	26									
Soft-plumaged Petrel	26									
Herald Petrel	26									
Kermadec Petrel	26									
Barau's Petrel	†									
White-headed Petrel	26									
White-necked Petrel	28									
Mottled Petrel	28									
Blue Petrel	28									
Cook's Petrel	28									
Black-winged Petrel	28									
Gould's Petrel	28									
Whalebird (Prion)	30									
broad-billed form										
medium-billed form										
Antarctic form										
Running Total										

† A recent addition to the Australian bird list.

1 2 3 4 5

	Page ref.*	Life-list								
slender-billed (thin-billed) form										
Prion	30									
Australian form										
Fulmar-like form										
Wedge-tailed Shearwater	32									
Fleshy-footed Shearwater	32									
Buller's Shearwater	32									
Streaked Shearwater	32									
Short-tailed Shearwater	32									
Sooty Shearwater	32									
Manx Shearwater	34									
Hutton's Shearwater	34									
Fluttering Shearwater	34									
Audubon's Shearwater	34									
Little Shearwater	34									
Wilson's Storm Petrel	38									
Leach's Storm Petrel	38									
Matsudaira's Storm Petrel	38									
White-bellied Storm Petrel	38, 40									
Bulwer's Petrel	38									
Black-bellied Storm Petrel	40									
Grey-backed Storm Petrel	40									
White-faced Storm Petrel	40									
Running Total										

CHECKLIST OF AUSTRALIAN BIRDS

		1	2	3	4	5							

	Page ref.*	Life-list	OCT 23/95 ✓	23	24	25 26	27	28 29
Common Diving Petrel	40							
Georgian Diving Petrel	40							
Australian Gannet	42							
Cape Gannet	42							
Masked Booby	42							
Brown Booby	42	✗						
Red-footed Booby	42							
Least (Lesser) Frigatebird	46	✗						
Great (Greater) Frigatebird	46							
Christmas Island Frigatebird	46							
Red-tailed Tropicbird	46							
White-tailed Tropicbird	46							
white form								
golden form								
✓ Little Pied Cormorant	48	NZ✓		✓				✓
✓ Little Black Cormorant	48	✓		✓				✓
✓ Australian Darter	48	✓						✓
✓ Great Cormorant	48	NI✓	✓					
Pied Cormorant	48							
Black-faced Shag	48							
✓ Australian Pelican	50	✗ ✓						✓
Great-billed Heron	50	✓						✓
Black-necked Stork (Jabiru)	50	✓						✓
Running Total								

30	31	1	2	3	4	5	6	7					
		✓					✓						
							✓						
✓							✓						
							✓						
							✗						
	✓						✓	✓					
	✓												

	Page ref.*	Life-list	OCT ✓ 23/95	23	24	25	'26	27 28	29
✓ Brolga	50	✓							✓
✓ Sarus Crane	50	✓							
✓ Cattle Egret	52	CAN ✓				✓			✓
✓ Eastern Reef Egret	52	✗							
dark phase									
white phase •									
✓ Little Egret	52	✗ ✓							✓
✓ Intermediate Egret	52	✗ ✓							✓
✓ Great Egret	52	✗ ✓							✓
✓ White-faced Heron	54	Nzy				✓			
✓ Pacific Heron	54	✓				✓			✓
Grey Heron	54								
✓ Pied Heron	54	✓							✓
✓ Rufous (Nankeen) Night Heron	54	✓							✓
✓ Striated (Mangrove) Heron	56	✓							
Little Bittern	56								
Yellow Bittern	56								
Black Bittern	56								
Australasian (Brown) Bittern	56								
✓ Royal Spoonbill	58	✓							✓
✓ Yellow-billed Spoonbill	58	✓							✓
✓ Straw-necked Ibis	58	✓				✓			✓
✓ Sacred Ibis (White)	58	✗ ✓				✓			✓
Running Total									

104

30 31 1 2 3 4 5 6 7 8

	Page ref.*	Life-list	23/5	23	24	25	26	27	28	29
Glossy Ibis	58	✓								✓
Burdekin Duck (Radjah Shelduck)	60	✓								✓
Australian Shelduck	60									
Cape Barren Goose	60									
Pied Goose	60	✓								✓
Black Swan	60	N-Z ✓				✓				
Mute Swan	60									
Plumed Whistling-duck	62	✓								✓
Wandering Whistling-duck	62	✓								✓
Freckled Duck	62									
Wood Duck	62	✓			✓	✓				
Hardhead	62	✓								
Red-crested Pochard	62									
Pacific Black Duck	64	N-Z ✓			✓	✓				
Mallard	64	✓								
Northern Shoveler	64									
Australasian Shoveler	64									
Pintail	†									
Australian Grey Teal	66	✓				✓				
Chesnut Teal	66									
Garganey	66									
Baikal Teal	66									
Green Pygmy-goose	68	✓								✓
Running Total										

† A recent addition to the Australian bird list.

CHECKLIST OF AUSTRALIAN BIRDS

30	31	1	2	3	4	5	6						
		✓											
✓	✓												
							✓						
	✓												
							✓						
	✓						✓						
	✓	✓											

	Page ref.*	Life-list	OCT 22/23	23	24	25	26	27	28	29
Cotton Pygmy-goose	68									
Pink-eared Duck	68									
Blue-billed Duck	68									
Musk Duck	68									
Collared Sparrowhawk	72									
Brown Goshawk	72									
temperate race										
tropical race										
Grey Goshawk	72									
grey phase										
white phase										
Red Goshawk	72									
Pacific Baza (Crested Hawk)	74									
Swamp Harrier	74	✗								
Spotted Harrier	74									
Papuan Harrier	74									
✓ Black Kite	76	✓				✓	✓			✓
Square-tailed Kite	76									
Black-breasted Buzzard (Kite)	76									
✓ Whistling Kite	76	✓				✓	✓			✓
✓ Brahminy Kite	76	✓								
White-eyed Buzzard	76									
✓ Osprey	78	CAN ✓								
Running Total										

CHECKLIST OF AUSTRALIAN BIRDS

30	31	1	2	3	4	5	6	7	8	9			
✓	✓			✓	✓	✓	✓						
								✓					
								✓					

	Page ref.*	Life-list	Oct 23/55	23	24	25	26	27	28	29
Little Eagle	78	✗								
light phase										
dark phase										
✓ White-breasted Sea-Eagle	78	✓								✓
✓ Wedge-tailed Eagle	78	✗✓					✓			
Letter-winged Kite	80									
✓ Black-shouldered Kite	80	✓							✓	✓
Black Falcon	80									
✓ Brown Falcon	80	✓		✓	✓	✓				✓
dark form										
red-breasted form										
sandy-breasted form										
grey-headed form										
speckle-breasted form										
stripe-breasted form										
white-breasted form										
✓ Australian (Nankeen) Kestrel	82	✓					✓			
Australian Hobby	82									
Grey Falcon	82									
Peregrine Falcon	82									
Malleefowl	86									
✓ Australian Brush-turkey	86	✓								
northern form										
Running Total										

CHECKLIST OF AUSTRALIAN BIRDS

30	31	1	2	3	4	5	6	7					
		✓				✓		✓					
	✓												
							✓						
		✓		✓		✓	✓						

111

	Page ref.*	Life-list	Oct 23/95	23	24	25	26	27	28	29
eastern form	86									
Orange-footed Scrubfowl	86									
Beach Thick-knee	86									
✓ Bush Thick-knee	86	✗ ✓								
Australian (Kori?) Bustard	86									
Painted Button-quail	88									
mainland form										
Houtman Abrolhos form										
Chestnut-backed Button-quail	88									
buff-breasted form										
grey-breasted form										
Brown Quail	88									
Stubble Quail	88									
King Quail	88									
Red-backed Button-quail	90									
eastern form										
northern form										
Red-chested Button-quail	90									
✓ Little Button-quail	90	✓					✓			
Black-breasted Button-quail	90									
Plains Wanderer	90									
Lewin's Rail	92									
Spotless Crake	92									
Running Total										

CHECKLIST OF AUSTRALIAN BIRDS

30	31	1	2	3	4	5	6						
	✓						✓						

113

	Page ref.*	Life-list	oct 23/95	23	24	25	26	'27		
Australian Crake	92									
Baillon's Crake	92									
Red-legged Crake	92									
✓ White-browed Crake	92	✓								
Buff-banded Rail	94									
Red-necked Crake	94									
Bush-hen	94									
Corncrake	94									
✓ Comb-crested Jacana	94	✓						✓		
Pheasant-tailed Jacana	94									
✓ Eurasian Coot	96	N.I				✓				
✓ Dusky Moorhen	96	✓		✓						
✓ Purple Swamphen	96	✓		✓						
south-western form										
eastern form										
✓ Black-tailed Native-hen	96	✓			✓					
Tasmanian Native-hen	96									
Chestnut Rail	96									
✓ Lesser Golden Plover	98	✓								
Pacific form										
American form										
Grey Plover	98									
Banded Lapwing	98									
Running Total										

CHECKLIST OF AUSTRALIAN BIRDS

30	31	1	2	3	4	5	6						
	✓												
							✓						
		✓					✓						
		✓				✓							
						✓							

	Page ref.*	Life-list	Oct. 23/95	23	24	25	26	27	28	29
✓ Masked Lapwing	98	✓				✓				✓
. eastern form										
northern form										
Red-kneed Dotterel	100									
Hooded Plover	100									
✓ Black-fronted Dotterel	100	✓				✓				✓
Inland Dotterel	100									
Caspian Plover	102									
Oriental Plover	102									
Large Sand-Plover	102									
✓ Mongolian Sand-Plover	102	✓								
Double-banded Plover	104									
Ringed Plover	104									
Little Ringed Plover	104									
✓ Red-capped Plover (Dotterel)	104	✓				✓				
✓ Red-necked Stint	108	✓								
Little Stint	108									
Long-toed Stint	108									
Western Sandpiper	108									
✓ Sanderling	110	✓								
Broad-billed Sandpiper	110									
White-rumped Sandpiper	110									
✓ Sharp-tailed Sandpiper	112	✓				✓				
Running Total										

CHECKLIST OF AUSTRALIAN BIRDS

30	31	1	2	3	4	5	6						
		✓			✓	✓	✓						
		✓											
							✓						
							✓						
							✓						
							✓						
							✓						

117

	Page ref.*	Life-list	22/55 23 24 25 26						
Pectoral Sandpiper	112								
Cox's Sandpiper	112								
Ruff	112								
Curlew Sandpiper	114								
Dunlin	114								
Stilt Sandpiper	114								
Buff-breasted Sandpiper	114								
✓ Grey-tailed Tattler	116	✓							
Wandering Tattler	116								
Red Knot	116								
✓ Great Knot	116	✓							
✓ Ruddy Turnstone	116	✓							
Latham's (Japanese) Snipe	118								
Swinhoe's Snipe	118								
Pintail Snipe	118								
Painted Snipe	118								
Asian Dowitcher	120								
✓ Bar-tailed Godwit	120	✓							
✓ Black-tailed Godwit	120	✓							
Hudsonian Godwit	120								
Little Curlew	122								
✓ Whimbrel	122	✓							
Asian form									
Running Total									

CHECKLIST OF AUSTRALIAN BIRDS

90 91 0 2 3 4 5 6

119

	Page ref.*	Life-list	23/95	23	24	25	26			
American form										
✓ Eastern Curlew	122	✗✓								
Eurasian Curlew	122									
Upland Sandpiper	124									
Marsh Sandpiper	124									
✓ Common Greenshank	124	✓								
Spotted Greenshank	124									
Lesser Yellowlegs	126									
Greater Yellowlegs	126									
Spotted Redshank	126									
Common Redshank	126									
Common Sandpiper	128									
✓ Wood Sandpiper	128	✓			✓					
Green Sandpiper	128									
✓ Terek Sandpiper	128	✗✓								
Australian Pratincole	130									
Oriental Pratincole	130									
Red-necked Phalarope	130									
Grey (Red) Phalarope	130									
Wilson's Phalarope	130									
Banded Stilt	132									
✓ Black-winged Stilt	132	✗✓			✓					
✓ Red-necked Avocet	132	✓			✓					
Running Total										

CHECKLIST OF AUSTRALIAN BIRDS

1 2 3 4 5 6

						✓							
						✓							
						✓							

THE BIRDWATCHER'S NOTEBOOK

	Page ref.*	Life-list	OCT 23/95	23	24	25	26	27	28	29
Pied Oystercatcher	132									
Sooty Oystercatcher	132									
Arctic Jaeger	134									
Pomarine Jaeger	134									
Long-tailed Jaeger	134									
Southern (Great) Skua	134									
Southern Polar Skua	134									
Pacific Gull	136									
Black-tailed Gull	136									
Lesser Black-backed Gull	136									
Kelp Gull	136									
Sabine's Gull	138									
Franklin's Gull	138									
Saunder's Gull	138									
Laughing Gull	†									
✓ Silver Gull	138	✓	✓	✓	✓					
White Tern	140									
✓ Gull-billed Tern	140	✓								
✓ Lesser Crested Tern	140	✓								
Crested Tern	140	✓								
✓ Caspian Tern	140	✓								
Little Tern	142									
Fairy Tern	142									
Running Total										

† A recent addition to the Australian bird list.

CHECKLIST OF AUSTRALIAN BIRDS

30	31	1	2	3	4	5	6	2	8				
				✓	✓		✓		✓				
							✓						
								✓					
							✗						
				✓	✓		✓						

123

	Page ref.*	Life-list	Oct 22/95	23	24	25	26			
✓ Black-naped Tern	142	✓								
Black Tern	142									
✓ White-winged [BLACK] Tern	142	✓			✓					✗✗
✓ Whiskered Tern	142	/								✓
Roseate Tern	146									
White-fronted Tern	146									
✓ Common Tern	146	✓								
eastern form										
European form										
Arctic Tern	146									
Antarctic Tern	146									
Sooty Tern	148									
Bridled Tern	148									
Common Noddy	148	✗								
White-capped Noddy	148	✗								
Lesser Noddy	148									
Grey Noddy (Ternlet)	148									
Squatter Pigeon	150									
southern form										
northern form										
✓ Partridge Pigeon	150	✓								
yellow-faced form										
red-faced form										
Running Total										

CHECKLIST OF AUSTRALIAN BIRDS

31	1	2	3	4	5	6	7	8				
							✗	✓				
						✓						
✓						✓						
						✓						
✓												

125

	Page ref.*	Life-list	OCT 23/95	23	24	25	26	27	28	29
Flock Bronzewing	150									
✓ Crested Pigeon	150	✓				✓				✓
Spinifex Pigeon	150									
reddish-bellied form										
white-bellied form										
Chestnut-quilled Rock-Pigeon	152									
White-quilled Rock-Pigeon	152									
Common Bronzewing	152									
Brush Bronzewing	152									
✓ Wonga Pigeon	152	✓								
✓ Feral Pigeon	152	✓		✓						✓
✓ Diamond Dove	154	+✓							✓	✓
✓ Peaceful Dove	154	×✓								✓
✓ Bar-shouldered Dove	154	✓								!
✓ Spotted Turtle-dove	154	×✗	✓	✓	✓					
Laughing Turtle-dove	154									
Emerald Dove	154									
northern form										
eastern form										
Superb Fruit-Dove	156									
Rose-crowned Fruit-Dove	156									
eastern form										
western form										
Running Total										

31	1	2	3	4	5	6					
	✓										
		✓									
			✓	✓		✓					
✓			✓		✓	✓					
✓											

	Page ref.*	Life-list	OCT 23/55	23	24	25	26			28
Wompoo Fruit-Dove	156	✓								
Brown Cuckoo-Dove	156	✓								
White-headed Pigeon	158									
Banded Fruit-Dove	158									
Torresian Imperial-Pigeon	158	✓								✓
Black-collared Imperial-Pigeon	158									
Topknot Pigeon	158	✓			✓					
Gang-gang Cockatoo	160									
Pink Cockatoo (Major Mitchell)	160									
Galah	160	✓				✓	✓			✓
Sulphur-crested Cockatoo	160	x✓		✓	✓					✓
Little Corella	160	✓				✓				✓
widespread form										
north-western form										
south-western form										
Long-billed Corella	160									
Yellow-tailed Black-Cockatoo	162									
large form										
small form										
Long-billed (Baudin's) Black-Cockatoo	162									
White-tailed (Carnaby's) Black-Cockatoo	162									
Glossy Black-Cockatoo	162									
Red-tailed Black-Cockatoo	162	✓					✓			
Running Total										

CHECKLIST OF AUSTRALIAN BIRDS

30	31	1	2	3	4	5	6	7					
			✓	✓									
		✓	✓	✓	✓	✓		✓					
					✓	✓							
		✓	✓		✓	✓							
		✓											
✓	✓						✓						

129

	Page ref.*	Life-list	oct 22/15	23	24	25	26	27	28 29
Palm Cockatoo	162								
Rainbow Lorikeet	164	✓							✓
eastern form									
red-collared form									
Scaly-breasted Lorikeet	164								
Swift Parrot	164								
Varied Lorikeet	164	✓							✓
Musk Lorikeet	166								
Little Lorikeet	166								
Purple-crowned Lorikeet	166								
Double-eyed Fig-Parrot	166								
Coxen's form									
Macleay's form									
Marshall's form									
King Parrot	168	✓							
Red-winged Parrot	168	✓							✓
Red-cheeked Parrot	168								
Cockatiel	168	✓				✓	✓		
Eclectus Parrot	168								
Ringneck (Ringnecked Parrot) (MALLEE)	170	✓				✓	✓		✓
Twenty-eight form									
Port Lincoln form									
mallee form									
Running Total									

3) 1 2 3 4 5 6

THE BIRDWATCHER'S NOTEBOOK

	Page ref.*	Life-list	22/95	23	24	25	26		
Cloncurry form									
Red-capped Parrot	170								
Princess Parrot	170								
Superb Parrot	170								
Regent Parrot	170								
White-cheeked Rosella	172								
eastern form									
pale-headed form									
Northern Rosella	172								
Western Rosella	172								
Green Rosella	172								
✓ Blue-cheeked ('Crimson') Rosella	172	✓		✓					
ᵉ crimson form									
yellow form									
Adelaide form									
Red-rumped Parrot	174								
Mulga Parrot	174								
Paradise Parrot	174								
Golden-shouldered Parrot	174								
Hooded Parrot	174								
Rock Parrot	176								
Elegant Parrot	176								
Blue-winged Parrot	176								
Running Total									

CHECKLIST OF AUSTRALIAN BIRDS

30	31	1	2	3	4	5							
			✓	✓	✓								

	Page ref.*	Life-list	OCT 23/95	'23	'24	'25	'26			
Orange-bellied Parrot	176									
Turquoise Parrot	176									
Scarlet-chested Parrot	176									
Blue Bonnet	178									
Budgerigar	178	✓				✓				
Bourke's Parrot	178									
Ground Parrot	178									
Night Parrot	178									
Chestnut-breasted Cuckoo	180									
Fan-tailed Cuckoo	180	✓			✓					
Brush Cuckoo	180	✓								✓
Oriental Cuckoo	180									
Pallid Cuckoo	180									
Shining (Golden) Bronze-Cuckoo	182									
golden form										
shining form										
Black-eared Cuckoo	182									
Horsfield's Bronze-Cuckoo	182									
Little Bronze-Cuckoo	182									
rufous-breasted form										
white-breasted form										
Pheasant Coucal	184	✓								✓
Channel-billed Cuckoo	184	✓								
Running Total										

134

30 31 1 2 3 4 5 6

OCT
23/95 23   24   25   26

	Page ref.*	Life-list	23/95	23	24	25	26		
✓ Common Koel	184	✓							✓
Long-tailed Koel	184								
✓ Blue-winged Kookaburra	184	✓							
✓ Laughing Kookaburra	184	✗✓			✓				
Collared (Mangrove) Kingfisher	186								
Sacred Kingfisher	186								
✓ Forest Kingfisher	186	✗✓			✓				✓
Yellow-billed Kingfisher	186								
✓ Red-backed Kingfisher	186	✓				✓			
Buff-breasted Paradise-Kingfisher	188								
Common Paradise-Kingfisher	188								
Little Kingfisher	188								
✓ Azure Kingfisher	188	✓							✓
✓ Rainbow Bee-eater	188	✓							
✓ Dollarbird	188	✗✓							✓
Barn Owl	190								
Masked Owl	190								
Sooty Owl	190								
Grass Owl	190								
Lesser Sooty Owl	190								
✓ Southern Boobook	192	✓							
Oriental Boobook (Brown Hawk-Owl)	192								
Barking Owl	192								
Running Total									

CHECKLIST OF AUSTRALIAN BIRDS

30	31	1	2	3	4	5	6	7					
✓	✓												
✓		✓		✓	✓	✓	✓	✓					
	✓				✓	✓		✓					
						✓							
					✓	✓							
✓							✓						
						✓							

137

	Page ref.*	Life-list	OCT 22/96	23	24	25	26			
Rufous Owl	192									
Powerful Owl	192									
Large-tailed Nightjar	194									
Spotted Nightjar	194									
White-throated Nightjar	194									
Australian Owlet-nightjar	194									
grey-bellied form										
white-bellied form										
✓Tawny Frogmouth	196	✓								
Marbled Frogmouth	196									
northern form										
southern form										
Papuan Frogmouth	196									
Glossy Swiftlet	198									
✓ White-rumped Swiftlet	198	*✓								
Uniform Swiftlet	198									
Fork-tailed Swift	198									
✓ White-throated Needletail	198	✓								
House Swift	198									
✓Welcome Swallow	200	N.Z ✓		✓	✓	✓				
Barn Swallow	200									
Red-rumped Swallow	200									
✓Fairy Martin	200	✓			✓			✓		
Running Total										

138

1 2 3 4 5 6 7

		✓	✓										
					✓	✓							
						✓							
		✓	✓		✓	✓	✓	✓					
					✓								

	Page ref.*	Life-list	23/95	23	24	25	26		28
✓ Tree Martin	200	✓				✓			✓
✓ White-backed Swallow	200	✓				✓			
Blue-winged Pitta	202								
Noisy Pitta	202								
Red-bellied Pitta	202								
✓ Rainbow Pitta	202	✓							
Russet Ground-Thrush	202								
Australian Ground-Thrush	202								
south-eastern form									
Atherton form									
Song Thrush	202								
Blackbird	—								
Rufous Scrub-bird	204								
Noisy Scrub-bird	204								
Eastern Bristlebird	204								
Western Bristlebird	204								
Rufous Bristlebird	204								
south-western form									
eastern form									
Yellow Wagtail	206								
Grey Wagtail	206								
Yellow-headed Wagtail	206								
White Wagtail	206								
Running Total									

CHECKLIST OF AUSTRALIAN BIRDS

30	31	1	2	3	4	5	6	7	8				
		✓						✓					
	✓												

	Page ref.*	Life-list	'22/'23	'23	24	25	26	27	28	29
Skylark	208									
Singing Bushlark	208									
Rufous Songlark	208									
✓ Richard's Pipit	208	N.Z. ✓					✓			
Brown Songlark	208									
Yellow-eyed (Barred) Cuckoo-shrike	210									
Ground Cuckoo-shrike	210									
✓ Black-faced Cuckoo-shrike	210	✗ ✓				✓	✓			✓
✓ White-bellied Cuckoo-shrike (LITTLE)	210	✗ ✓								
eastern form										
northern form										
✓ White-winged Triller	212	✓					✓		✓	
✓ Varied Triller	212	✓								✓
eastern form										
Cape York form										
northern form										
Cicadabird	212									
✓ Red-whiskered Bulbul	212	✓			✓					
Red-vented Bulbul	212									
Pink Robin	214									
Rose Robin	214									
✓ Red-capped Robin	214	✓					✓			
Flame Robin	214									
Running Total										

CHECKLIST OF AUSTRALIAN BIRDS

3)	1	2	3	4	5	6	7					
	✓		✓		✓	✓	✓					
✓	✓		✓			✓						
	✓				✓	✓						

143

THE BIRDWATCHER'S NOTEBOOK

	Page ref.*	Life-list	αΓ 23/98	23	24	25	26			
Scarlet Robin	214									
White-browed Robin	216									
white-sided form										
buff-sided form										
Mangrove Robin	216									
Hooded Robin	216									
Dusky Robin	216									
✓ Grey-headed Robin	216	✓								
✓ Eastern Yellow Robin	218	ᴺᶻ✓		✓						
north-eastern form										
✓ PALE-YELLOW ROBIN south-eastern form		✓								
Western Yellow Robin	218									
White-breasted Robin	218									
southern form										
northern form										
White-faced Robin	218									
Yellow-legged Flycatcher	220									
Brown Flycatcher (Jacky Winter)	220									
✓ Lemon-bellied ᵃ ᵂ ᴮᴼᴬᵀ (-breasted) Flycatcher	220	✓						✓		
Cape York form										
lemon-bellied form										
white-bellied form										
Southern Scrub-Robin	220									
Running Total										

144

CHECKLIST OF AUSTRALIAN BIRDS

30	31	1	2	3	4	5	6	7					
					✓		✓						
			✓				✓						
		✓	✓			✓	✓	✓					

	Page ref.*	Life-list	oct 22/96	23	24	25	26			
Northern Scrub-Robin	220									
Crested Shrike-tit	222									
eastern form										
northern form										
south-western form										
✓ Golden Whistler	222	✓		✓						
Olive Whistler	222									
Mangrove Golden Whistler northern/eastern form	222									
western form										
✓ Grey Whistler	224	✓								
yellow-bellied form										
brown form										
White-breasted Whistler	224									
✓ Rufous Whistler	224	✓					✓			
Gilbert's Whistler	224									
Red-lored Whistler	224									
✓ Little (Rufous) Shrike-thrush	226	✓								
rufous form										
black-billed form										
Bower's Shrike-thrush	226									
✓ Grey Shrike-thrush	226	✓					✓			
eastern/northern form										
Running Total										

30 31 1 2 3 4 5 6

			✓									
					✓							
	✓											
			✓									
			✓				✓					
	✓		✓									

THE BIRDWATCHER'S NOTEBOOK

	Page ref.*	Life-list	OCT 22/88	23	24	25	26			29
western form										
Crested Bellbird	226									
Sandstone Shrike-thrush	226									
✓Shining Flycatcher	228	✓								✓
✓Spectacled Monarch	228	✓								
white-bellied form										
buff-bellied form										
✓Black-faced Monarch	228	✓		✗✓	✓					
Black-winged Monarch	228									
✓ Pied Monarch	230	✓								
Frilled Monarch	230									
✓White-eared Monarch	230	✓								
✓ Yellow-breasted Boatbill	230	✓								
✓Restless Flycatcher	232	✗✓								✓
southern form										
northern form										
✓ Satin Flycatcher	232	✗								
✓ Broad-billed Flycatcher	232	✓								
✓Leaden Flycatcher	232	✓	✓	✓						
✓ Grey Fantail	234	N.T.	✗✓	✓						✓
southern forms										
white-tailed form										
mountain form										
Running Total										

CHECKLIST OF AUSTRALIAN BIRDS

30	31	1	2	3	4	5	6						
✓	✓												
	✓		✓			✓							
	✓		✓	✓			✓						
					✓								
							✓						
							✓						
	✓												
	✓												
✓	✓												
	✓		✓			✓	✓						
✓													

149

	Page ref.*	Life-list	2/55	23	24	25	26		29
Mangrove Fantail	234								
✓ Rufous Fantail	234	✓							
✓ Northern Fantail	234	✓							✓
✓ Willy Wagtail	234	✓			✓	✓	✓		✓
Western Whipbird	236								
western form									
eastern form									
✓ Eastern Whipbird	236	✓			✓				
south-eastern form									
north Queensland form									
Chiming Wedgebill	236								
Chirruping Wedgebill	236								
✓ Logrunner	236	✓							
✓ Chowchilla	236	✓							
Chestnut-breasted Quail-thrush	238								
eastern form									
western form									
Nullarbor Quail-thrush	238								
Cinnamon Quail-thrush	238								
Chestnut Quail-thrush	238								
Spotted Quail-thrush	238								
Chestnut-crowned Babbler	240								
Hall's Babbler	240								
Running Total									

30	31	1	2	3	4	5	6	7					
		✓	✓										
✓	✓												
✓	✓				✓	✓	✓						
			✓										
		✓											
					✓								

	Page ref.*	Life-list	OCT 23/95	23	24	25	26	27	28	
White-browed Babbler	240									
✓ Grey-crowned Babbler	240	✓								
grey-breasted form										
red-breasted form										
Gray's Grasshopper Warbler	242									
Great Reed-Warbler	242									
✓ Australian (Clamorous) Reed-Warbler	242	✓			✓					
Tawny Grassbird	242									
Little Grassbird	242									
Spinifexbird	242									
Zitting Cisticola	244									
✓ Golden-headed Cisticola	244	✓						?✓→		
Mallee Emu-wren	244									
Rufous-crowned Emu-wren	244									
Southern Emu-wren	244									
✓ Superb Fairy-wren	246	✓								
Purple-crowned Fairy-wren	246									
western form										
eastern form										
✓ Splendid Fairy-wren	246	✓						✓		
western form										
turquoise form										
black-backed form										
Running Total										

CHECKLIST OF AUSTRALIAN BIRDS

30	31	1	2	3	4	5							
✓	✓												
	✓				✓								

	Page ref.*	Life-list	Oct 23/95	23	24	25	26			29
White-winged Fairy-wren	246	✓				✓♀				
blue and white form										
black and white form										
Lovely Fairy-wren	248									
violet-headed form										
blue-headed form										
Blue-breasted Fairy-wren	248									
Red-winged Fairy-wren	248									
✓ Variegated Fairy-wren	248	✓			✓					
✓ Red-backed Fairy-wren	248	✓								
scarlet-backed form										
crimson-backed form										
Dusky Grasswren	250									
Purnell's form										
Horton's form										
Thick-billed Grasswren	250									
short-tailed central form										
long-tailed western form										
White-throated Grasswren	250									
Black Grasswren	250									
Grey Grasswren	252									
Eyrean Grasswren	252									
Carpentarian Grasswren	252									
Running Total										

CHECKLIST OF AUSTRALIAN BIRDS

3| 1 2 3 4 5 1 7

					✓		✓					

155

	Page ref.*	Life-list	22/95	23	24	25	26			
Striated Grasswren	252									
mallee form										
short-tailed form										
sandhill form										
Pilbara form										
✓White-browed Scrubwren	254	✓			✓					
spotted form										
south-eastern form										
Tasmanian form										
buff-breasted form										
McPherson Range form										
Scrub-tit	254									
✓Yellow-throated Scrubwren	254	✓								
Australian Fernwren	254									
Tropical Scrubwren	256									
northern form										
southern form										
✓Atherton Scrubwren	256	✓								
✓Large-billed Scrubwren	256	✓								
Redthroat	256									
Pilotbird	256									
✓ Rock Warbler (Origma)	256	✓			✓					
Speckled Warbler	258									
Running Total										

CHECKLIST OF AUSTRALIAN BIRDS

31	1	2	3	4	5	6						
		✓	✓									
		✓			✓							
				✓								
	✓	✓			✓							

	Page ref.*	Life-list	OCT 23/26	23	24	25	26			
Chestnut-rumped Heathwren (Hylacola)	258									
Shy Heathwren (Hylacola)	258									
Striated Fieldwren (Calamanthus)	258									
Rufous Fieldwren (Calamanthus)	258									
southern form										
mid-western form										
north-western form										
Brown Warbler (Gerygone)	260	✓								
southern form										
northern form										
Mangrove Warbler (Gerygone)	260									
eastern form										
northern form										
Western Warbler (Gerygone)	260									
Green-backed Warbler (Gerygone)	260									
Dusky Warbler (Gerygone)	260									
Large-billed Warbler (Gerygone)	262									
Rusty-tailed Warbler (Gerygone)	262									
✓ Fairy Warbler (Gerygone) (PALPEBROSA)	262	✓								
southern form										
intermediate form										
northern form										
White-throated Warbler (Gerygone)	262									
Running Total										

CHECKLIST OF AUSTRALIAN BIRDS

30			2	3	4	5	6						
			✓	✓									
					✓								

	Page ref.*	Life-list	23/95	23	24	25	26			
Arctic Warbler	262									
✓ Striated Thornbill	264	✓		✓						
Yellow Thornbill	264									
✓ Weebill	264	✓			✓					
southern form										
northern form										
south-western form										
Southern Whiteface	264									
western form										
eastern form										
Chestnut-breasted Whiteface	264									
Banded Whiteface	264									
Buff-rumped Thornbill	266									
southern form										
northern form										
Western Thornbill	266									
Slender-billed (Samphire) Thornbill	266									
Iredale's form										
Rosina's form										
Hedley's form										
Yellow-rumped Thornbill	266									
Chestnut-rumped Thornbill	266									
✓ Mountain Thornbill	266	✓								
Running Total										

30	31	Nov Dec 1	2	3	4	5	6						
			✓										
							✓						

	Page ref.*	Life-list	OC 23/95	23	24	25	26			
✓ Brown Thornbill	268	✓			✓					
broad-tailed form										
Tanami form										
Yellow-bellied form										
white-bellied form										
south-eastern form										
south-western form										
Tasmanian form										
King Island form										
Tasmanian Thornbill	268									
Slate-backed Thornbill	268									
✓ Varied Sittella	270	✓			✓					
striated form										
white-winged form										
black-capped form										
orange-winged form										
white-headed form										
pied form										
Black-tailed Treecreeper	270									
north-western form										
northern form										
Rufous Treecreeper	270									
White-throated Treecreeper	272	✓			✓					
Running Total										

CHECKLIST OF AUSTRALIAN BIRDS

		1	2	3	4	5								
		✓	✓	✓										
		✓	✓	✓										

	Page ref.*	Life-list	23/95	23	24	25	26			29
large form										
small form (Little)										
Eungella form										
Red-browed Treecreeper	272									
White-browed Treecreeper	272									
Brown Treecreeper	272									
brown-backed form										
black-backed form										
✓ Spiny-cheeked Honeyeater	274	✓				✓	✓			
Yellow Wattlebird	274									
✓ Red Wattlebird	274	✗								
✓ Little Wattlebird	274	✓		✓						
Brush Wattlebird	—									
✓ Little Friarbird	276	✓								✓
✓ Helmeted Friarbird	276	✗✓								
✓ Silver-crowned Friarbird	276	✓								
✓ Noisy Friarbird	276	✓								
✓ Blue-faced Honeyeater	278	✓								
northern form										
eastern form										
✓ Yellow-throated Miner	278	✓				✓	✓			✓
white-rumped form										
black-eared form										
Running Total										

CHECKLIST OF AUSTRALIAN BIRDS

30	31	1	2	3	4	5	6	7					
	✓												
					✓								
✓													
						✓	✓						
✓	✓												
	✓												
	✓												

165

	Page ref.*	Life-list	23/95	23	24	25	26		29
dusky form									
✓ Noisy Miner	278	✓		?					
Bell Miner	278								
✗ ✓ White-throated Honeyeater	280	✓							✓
White-naped Honeyeater	280								
eastern form									
south-western form									
Brown-headed Honeyeater	280	?		?					
Black-headed Honeyeater	280								
Strong-billed Honeyeater	280								
Black-chinned Honeyeater	280								
eastern form									
northern form									
✓ Lewin's Honeyeater	282	✓		✓					
✓ Yellow-spotted Honeyeater	282	✓							
✓ Graceful Honeyeater	282	✓							
✓ White-gaped Honeyeater	282	✓							
White-lined Honeyeater	282								
✓ Bridled Honeyeater	282	✓							
Eungella Honeyeater	282								
Yellow-tufted Honeyeater	284								
helmeted form									
olive-crowned form									
Running Total									

CHECKLIST OF AUSTRALIAN BIRDS

30	31	1	2	3	4	5	6						
		✓	✓										
✓					✓								
		✓	✓	✓			✓						
						✓							
						✓							
✓	✓												
						✓							

167

	Page ref.*	Life-list	23	24	25	26	27	28	29
Yellow-throated Honeyeater	284								
Yellow Honeyeater	284								
White-eared Honeyeater	284	?		?					
✓ Yellow-faced Honeyeater	284	✓		✓					
✓ Varied Honeyeater	286	✓							
southern 'mangrove' form									
northern form									
✓ Singing Honeyeater	286	✓				✓			
Purple-gaped Honeyeater	286								
✓ Grey-headed Honeyeater	286	✓						✓	
Grey-fronted Honeyeater	288								
grey-fronted form									
olive-fronted form									
Yellow-plumed Honeyeater	288								
✓ White-plumed Honeyeater	288	✓		✓	✓	✓			✓
Fuscous Honeyeater	288								
Yellow-tinted Honeyeater	288								
Crescent Honeyeater	290								
✓ White-fronted Honeyeater	290	✓				✓			
✓ New Holland Honeyeater	290	✓		✓					
✓ White-cheeked Honeyeater	290	✓							
western form									
eastern form									
Running Total									

30   1 2 3 4 5 6

✓

✓

	Page ref.*	Life-list	23/95	23	24	25	26	27	28	29
Painted Honeyeater	290									
Regent Honeyeater	290									
✓ Bar-breasted Honeyeater	292	✓								
✓ Brown-backed Honeyeater	292	✓								
Rufous-throated Honeyeater	292									
✓ Rufous-banded Honeyeater	292	✓								
✓ Tawny-crowned Honeyeater	292	✓		✓						
Grey Honeyeater	292									
✓ Dusky Honeyeater	294	✓						✓		
✓ Scarlet Honeyeater	294	✓								
Red-headed Honeyeater	294									
✓ Eastern Spinebill	294	✓		✓						
Western Spinebill	294									
Black Honeyeater	296									
Banded Honeyeater	296									
Pied Honeyeater	296									
Tawny-breasted Honeyeater	296									
Macleay's Honeyeater	296									
Green-backed Honeyeater	298									
✓ Brown Honeyeater	298	✓							✓	
White-streaked Honeyeater	298									
Striped Honeyeater	298									
✓ Yellow-bellied Sunbird	298	✗✓								
Running Total										

30	31	1	2	3	4	5	6	7					
	✓				✗								
					✓								
	✓												
	✓				✓	✓	✓	✓					
			✓	✓									
	✓		✓	✓		✓		✓					
✓													
					✓	✓							

	Page ref.*	Life-list	23/05	23	24	25	26			29
Pale White-eye	300									
Yellow White-eye	300									
✓ Silvereye	300	✗	✓	✓						
Barrier Reef form										
↝ south-eastern forms										
Tasmanian form										
western form										
✓ Mistletoebird	300	✓			✓					
White-fronted Chat	302									
Gibber Chat	302									
Orange Chat	302									
Yellow Chat	302									
Crimson Chat	302									
✓ Spotted Pardalote	304	✓								
red-rumped form										
yellow-rumped form										
Forty-spotted Pardalote	304									
✓ Red-browed Pardalote	304	✓				✓				
typical form										
Gulf form										
Striated Pardalote	304									
yellow-rumped form										
cinnamon-rumped form										
Running Total										

172

30	31	1	2	3	4	5	6						
		✓	✓	✓									
	✓												
			✓										

THE BIRDWATCHER'S NOTEBOOK

	Page ref.*	Life-list	22/56	23	24	25	26	27	28	29
western form										
south-eastern form										
yellow-spotted form										
Star Finch	306									
Red-browed Firetail	306	a✓			✓					
Painted Firetail	306	✓							✓	
Diamond Firetail	306									
Red-eared Firetail	306									
Beautiful Firetail	306									
Double-barred Finch	308	✓								
white-rumped form										
black-rumped form										
Plum-headed Finch	308									
Blue-faced Finch	308									
Crimson Finch	308	✓								✓
white-bellied form										
black-bellied form										
Gouldian Finch	308									
Masked Finch	310									
white-eared form										
brown-eared form										
Long-tailed Finch	310									
yellow-billed form ZEBRA FINCH		✓				✓	✓			✓
Running Total										

174

CHECKLIST OF AUSTRALIAN BIRDS

30		1	2	3	4	5	6					
						✓						
					✓							
✓					✓							
					✓							
					✗							

175

	Page ref.*	Life-list	oct 22/95	23	24	25	26			29
red-billed form										
Black-throated Finch	310									
white-rumped form										
black-rumped form										
Yellow-rumped Mannikin	310									
✓ Chestnut-breasted Mannikin	310	✓								
Pictorella Mannikin	310									
x✓ Nutmeg Mannikin (Spice Finch)	312	✓								
Black-headed Mannikin	312									
European Goldfinch	312									
Greenfinch	312									
Tree Sparrow	312									
✓ House Sparrow	312	✓				✓				
White-winged Wydah	312									
Red Bishop (Grenadier Weaver)	312									
✓ Common Starling	314	✓				✓				
✓ Metallic Starling	314	✓								
Singing Starling	†									
✓ Yellow Oriole	314	✓								✓
Olive-backed Oriole	314									
✓ Figbird	314	x✓								
southern form										
intergrade										
Running Total										

† A recent addition to the Australian bird list.

CHECKLIST OF AUSTRALIAN BIRDS

30	31.	1	2	3	4	5	6	7					
						✓							
					✓								
			✓		✓	✓ ✓							
					✓ ✓								
	✓												
	✓				✓	✓	✓						

177

	Page ref.*	Life-list	22/95	23	24	25	26	27	28
northern form									
✓ Common Myna	316	× ✓	✓	✓	✓				
✓ Spangled Drongo	316	× ✓							
✓ Magpie-lark	316	✓	✓	✓	✓	✓	✓		
White-winged Chough	316								
Apostlebird	316								
✓ Little Woodswallow	318	✓							✓
Dusky Woodswallow	318								
✓ Black-faced Woodswallow	318	✓					✓		✓
black-vented form									
white-vented form									
✓ Masked Woodswallow	318	✓					✓		
✓ White-browed Woodswallow	318	✓					✓		
✓ White-breasted Woodswallow	318	✓							✓
Black-backed Butcherbird	320								
✓ Pied Butcherbird	320	✓						✓	
✓ Grey Butcherbird	320	✓							
southern/eastern form									
silver-backed form									
Kimberley form									
Tasmanian form									
✓ Black Butcherbird	320	✓							
✓ Pied Currawong	322	× ✓	✓	✓					
Running Total									

30   2 3 4 5 6 7 8

30				2	3	4	5	6	7	8			
					✓	✓	✓	✓	✓	✓			
✓				✓		✓	✓	✓					
	✓			✓	✓	✓	✓	✓					
	✓				✓	✓	✓						
	✗							✓					
	✗	✓	✓	✓									
					✓	✓							
	-	✓	✓	✓									

	Page ref.*	Life-list	OCT 23/95	23	24	25	26			
Grey Currawong	322									
brown form										
clinking form										
widespread form										
black-winged form										
Black Currawong	322									
Australian Magpie [N.Z.]	324	✓		✓	✓					
Papuan form										
white-backed form										
black-backed form										
Western form										
Tasmanian form										
✓Green Catbird	326	✓								
✓Spotted Catbird	326	✓								
Spotted Bowerbird	326	.								
Western Bowerbird	326									
✓Great Bowerbird	326	✓								
Fawn-breasted Bowerbird	326									
✓ Regent Bowerbird	328	✓ (M.)								
✓Tooth-billed Catbird	328	✓								
✓Golden Bowerbird	328	✓								
✓ Satin Bowerbird	328	✓		✓						
small northern form										
Running Total										

CHECKLIST OF AUSTRALIAN BIRDS

30			1	2	3	4	5	6	7					
			✓	✓		✓		✓						
		✓												
						✓								
✓														
				✓										
							✓							
						✓								
✓			✓	✓		✓								

	Page ref.*	Life-list	OCT 23/55	23	24	25	26			
large southern form										
Magnificent Riflebird	330									
✓ Victoria's Riflebird	330	✓								
✓ Paradise Riflebird	330	✓								
Trumpet Manucode	330									
✓ Superb Lyrebird	332	✓		✓						
south-eastern form										
Prince Edward's form										
Albert's Lyrebird	332									
✓ Torresian Crow	334	✓			✓		✓			
✓ Little Crow	334	✓	.	✓						
House Crow	334									
Forest Raven	334									
Little Raven	334									
✓ Australian Raven	334	✓								
Running Total										

CHECKLIST OF AUSTRALIAN BIRDS

3✓			2	3	4	5	6	7				
							✓	✓	✓				
			✓										
	✓		✓									
		✓										

INDEX FOR CHECKLIST

DATE   PLACE

1. ———————————————
2. ———————————————
3. ———————————————
4. ———————————————
5. ———————————————
6. ———————————————
7. ———————————————
8. ———————————————
9. ———————————————
10. ———————————————
11. ———————————————
12. ———————————————
13. ———————————————
14. ———————————————
15. ———————————————
16. ———————————————
17. ———————————————
18. ———————————————
19. ———————————————
20. ———————————————
21. ———————————————
22. ———————————————
23. ———————————————
24. ———————————————
25. ———————————————
26. ———————————————
27. ———————————————
28. ———————————————
29. ———————————————
30. ———————————————

INDEX FOR CHECKLIST

DATE   PLACE

31. _____
32. _____
33. _____
34. _____
35. _____
36. _____
37. _____
38. _____
39. _____
40. _____
41. _____
42. _____
43. _____
44. _____
45. _____
46. _____
47. _____
48. _____
49. _____
50. _____
51. _____
52. _____
53. _____
54. _____
55. _____
56. _____
57. _____
58. _____
59. _____
60. _____

RELATIVE ABUNDANCE

PLACE						
DATE						
SPECIES						
TOTAL						

RELATIVE ABUNDANCE

DATE

									Rel. Abund- ance (%)

NEST RECORD CHART

SPECIES	Building		Eggs Laid					Hatch	Fledge
	Start	Finish	1	2	3	4	5		

MIGRANT ARRIVALS AND DEPARTURES

PLACE						
	Year		Year		Year	
SPECIES	Arr.	Dep.	Arr.	Dep.	Arr.	Dep.

DATE: PLACE:

WEATHER:

HABITAT:

_____

_____

_____

_____

_____

_____

_____

_____

_____

_____

_____

_____

_____

_____

_____

_____

_____

_____

_____

_____

_____

_____

DATE: PLACE:

WEATHER:

HABITAT:

NOTES

DATE: PLACE:
WEATHER:
HABITAT:

_____

_____

_____

_____

_____

_____

_____

_____

_____

_____

_____

_____

_____

_____

_____

_____

_____

_____

_____

_____

_____

DATE: PLACE:

WEATHER:

HABITAT:

DATE: PLACE:

WEATHER:

HABITAT:

_____

_____

_____

_____

_____

_____

_____

_____

_____

_____

_____

_____

_____

_____

_____

_____

_____

_____

_____

_____

_____

DATE: PLACE:

WEATHER:

HABITAT:

DATE: PLACE:

WEATHER:

HABITAT:

_____

_____

_____

_____

_____

_____

_____

_____

_____

_____

_____

_____

_____

_____

_____

_____

_____

_____

_____

_____

_____

_____

_____

_____

NOTES

DATE: PLACE:
WEATHER:
HABITAT:

DATE: PLACE:
WEATHER:
HABITAT:

_____
_____
_____
_____
_____
_____
_____
_____
_____
_____
_____
_____
_____
_____
_____
_____
_____
_____
_____
_____
_____
_____
_____

NOTES

DATE: PLACE:
WEATHER:
HABITAT:

NOTES

DATE: PLACE:
WEATHER:
HABITAT:

_____
_____
_____
_____
_____
_____
_____
_____
_____
_____
_____
_____
_____
_____
_____
_____
_____
_____
_____
_____
_____
_____
_____
_____

DATE: PLACE:

WEATHER:

HABITAT:

DATE: PLACE:
WEATHER:
HABITAT:

_____
_____
_____
_____
_____
_____
_____
_____
_____
_____
_____
_____
_____
_____
_____
_____
_____
_____
_____
_____
_____
_____

DATE: PLACE:
WEATHER:
HABITAT:

NOTES

DATE: PLACE:
WEATHER:
HABITAT:

_____
_____
_____
_____
_____
_____
_____
_____
_____
_____
_____
_____
_____
_____
_____
_____
_____
_____
_____
_____
_____

DATE: PLACE:

WEATHER:

HABITAT:

NOTES

DATE: PLACE:

WEATHER:

HABITAT:

_____

_____

_____

_____

_____

_____

_____

_____

_____

_____

_____

_____

_____

_____

_____

_____

_____

_____

_____

_____

_____

_____

_____

NOTES

DATE: PLACE:

WEATHER:

HABITAT:

NOTES

DATE: PLACE:

WEATHER:

HABITAT:

_____

_____

_____

_____

_____

_____

_____

_____

_____

_____

_____

_____

_____

_____

_____

_____

_____

_____

_____

_____

_____

NOTES

DATE: PLACE:

WEATHER:

HABITAT:

NOTES

DATE: PLACE:

WEATHER:

HABITAT:

_____

_____

_____

_____

_____

_____

_____

_____

_____

_____

_____

_____

_____

_____

_____

_____

_____

_____

_____

_____

_____

_____

NOTES

DATE: PLACE:

WEATHER:

HABITAT:

NOTES

DATE: PLACE:
WEATHER:
HABITAT:

_____
_____
_____
_____
_____
_____
_____
_____
_____
_____
_____
_____
_____
_____
_____
_____
_____
_____
_____
_____
_____
_____

NOTES

DATE: PLACE:

WEATHER:

HABITAT:

NOTES

DATE: PLACE:
WEATHER:
HABITAT:

_____

_____

_____

_____

_____

_____

_____

_____

_____

_____

_____

_____

_____

_____

_____

_____

_____

_____

_____

_____

_____